THE SAND HUTTON LIGHT RAILWAY

K.E.Hartley

Narrow Gauge Railway Society
Special issue of THE NARROW GAUGE No. 95/96

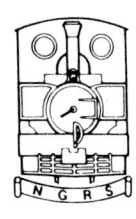

NARROW GAUGE RAILWAY SOCIETY

Serving the narrow gauge world since 1951

SECRETARY : M. Portsmouth, 15 Ham View, Upton-on-Severn, Worcs. WR8 0QE
MEMBERSHIP SECRETARY : P.A.Slater, The Hole in the Wall, Bradley, Ashbourne, Derbys.
TREASURER : J.H.Steele, 32 Thistley Hough, Penkhull, Stoke-on-Trent, ST4 5HU

The Society was founded in 1951 to encourage interest in all forms of narrow gauge rail transport. Members interests cover every aspect of the construction, operation, history and modelling of narrow gauge railways throughout the world. Society members receive this magazine and Narrow Gauge News, a bi-monthly review of current events on the narrow gauge scene. An extensive library, locomotive records, and modelling information service are available to members. Meetings and visits are arranged by local areas based in Leeds, Leicester, London, Malvern, Stoke-on-Trent and Warrington. Annual subscription currently £6.00, due 1st April.

THE NARROW GAUGE

EDITOR : M. Swift, 47 Birchington Avenue, Birchencliffe, Huddersfield, HD3 3RD
BACK NUMBER SALES : P.A. Salter, The Hole in the Wall, Bradley, Ashbourne, Derbys.
A. Neale, 7 Vinery Road, Leeds, LS4 2LB

Published quarterly by the Narrow Gauge Railway Society to record the history and development of narrow gauge rail transport. Our intention is to present a balanced, well illustrated publication, and the Editor welcomes original articles, photographs and drawings for consideration. Articles should preferably be written or typed with double spacing on one side of the paper only. The Editor appreciates a stamped addressed envelope if a reply is required. A range of back numbers, and binders for eight issues are available from the address above.

Copyright of all material in this magazine remains vested in the authors and publisher. Reproduction of whole or part of this magazine by any process is forbidden without the written permission of the Editor.

Printed by Hadfield Print Services Limited, Rassbottom Industrial Estate, Stalybridge, Cheshire SK15 1RH.

© Kenneth E. Hartley 1982

First edition published by the Narrow Gauge Railway Society, 1964.
This edition, revised and enlarged, published by the Narrow Gauge Railway Society,
47 Birchington Avenue, Birchencliffe. Huddersfield, West Yorkshire, HD3 3RD.

ISSN 0142-5587
ISBN 0 9507169 1 X

Cover upper: On the Sand Hutton Railway before the 1914-18 War SYNOLDA, with George Batty at the controls, stands outside the Garden Station depot with a train of four-wheeled coaches. (K.E. Hartley collection)

lower: Nearly fifteen years later on the Sand Hutton Light Railway No.12, hauling a typical passenger train, poses on the line between the Depot and Sand Hutton Central before proceeding to Warthill. George Batty is again at the controls. (H.G.W. Household)

CONTENTS

Preface 5
Acknowledgements 5
Introduction 7
Chapters:

1	The Sand Hutton Miniature Railway, 1912-14	9
2	The Bassett-Lowke 4-4-2 and SYNOLDA	12
3	15in gauge rolling stock	15
4	15in gauge line, 1914-20	17
5	The Light Railway Order	21
6	The Sand Hutton Light Railway	24
7	18in gauge locomotives	38
8	18in gauge passenger stock	43
9	18in gauge goods stock	47
10	Traffic and operation	51
11	The end of the line	56
12	Sand Hutton personalities	59
13	Present day	61

Appendix 1: Sand Hutton Light Railway — Traffic 64
Appendix 2: Sand Hutton Light Railway — Running Costs and Receipts 64
Bibliography 64

Maps and plans:
        Sand Hutton Miniature Railway — Map 8
        Sand Hutton Miniature Railway — Gradient profile 10
        Sand Hutton Light Railway — Map 28
        Sand Hutton Light Railway — Gradient profile 29
        Warthill Station and exchange sidings 31
        Sand Hutton Depot and Bossall Terminus 36

Drawings:
        Proposed 15in gauge 2-8-4T locomotive 18
        Proposed 15in gauge bogie wagons 20
        18in gauge bogie coach — side elevation and plan 32
        18in gauge bogie coach — end elevation 45
        18in gauge 0-4-0WT locomotive 40
        18in gauge open wagon 48
        18in gauge brake van 50

Seventy years after the birth of the Sand Hutton Railway, SYNOLDA stands at Dalegarth with a Narrow Gauge Railway Society special train for Ravenglass on 2nd May 1982.

The outward journey had been remarkable, which accounts for the satisfied smiles, but the return trip was exhilarating and proved that, far from being an elderly lady, SYNOLDA was capable of an amazing turn of speed with a well-filled three-coach train. *(V. Nutton)*

Preface

Eighteen years have elapsed since the original edition of *The Sand Hutton Light Railway* was published, and it has long been out of print. However, interest in this unique narrow gauge railway continues, and a steady demand for copies, together with certain fresh information which has become available in recent years, requires that a new edition should be produced to bring the history up-to-date and also to include a larger selection of illustrations, certain of which have not previously been published.

It is extremely unfortunate that World War II, with its "Salvage" drive, should have caused the destruction of old papers and records—thought to be of no further interest. But it is even more grieving to learn that complete plans of the railway, together with magazines, many photographs and other documents, should have survived intact until as recently as 1954, and then finally have been destroyed.

Not all, however, is on the debit side, for the respective builders of the locomotives, coaches and wagons have fortunately been able to supply copies of their drawings or detailed information. Furthermore, a rather surprising number of interesting photographs and snapshots have come to light. Not all, by any means, can be included in this booklet, but the present selection of photographs can be taken as fully representative, and will convey a good idea of how the Sand Hutton appeared both as a miniature railway and, later, as a true narrow gauge light railway.

Selby, North Yorkshire
February, 1982

Kenneth E. Hartley

Acknowledgements

The compilation of this book would have been impossible were it not for the willing and generous assistance which has been forthcoming from many directions. My sincere and grateful thanks are tendered to the Editors of *The Railway Magazine* and *The Locomotive,* and to Bassett-Lowke Ltd for permission to use material and illustrations from their pages; to The Hunslet Engine Co Ltd, Robert Hudson (Raletrux) Ltd, Leeds, and P. & W. MacLellan Ltd, for copies of drawings and other help; to British Railways, the City of York Reference Library, and the Ordnance Survey Dept., for information and assistance; and to the following firms and private individuals who have helped in a variety of ways:

Crust, Todd Mills & Co (Solicitors); W.J.N. Bryce (County Surveyor, East Riding County Council); N. Higson (County Archivist, East Riding County Council); G.A.W. Heppell (Flaxton Rural District Council); R. Sawtell (County Surveyor, North Riding County Council); Thos. W. Ward Ltd; World's Fair; Yorkshire Evening Post; Mrs. M. Abbey; M.H. Billington; J.I.C. Boyd; R. Bridge; D.J.W. Brough; R. Butterell; E.G. Cope; W.J.K. Davies; R.R. Dunn; D. Ferriera; L. Harrison; K. Hoole; D. Holroyde; R.J. Hunter; E.N. Jones; T.E. Jones (R.&E.R.); F. Jux; C.F. Klapper; A. Leadhill; H. Leadhill; J.C. Leeming; B. McFarlane; O. McNeil; B.J. Midgley; O.J. Morris; A. Neale; P. le Neve-Foster; H.E. Oakland; G.W. Pearson; K.P. Plant; Dr. P. Ransome-Wallis; S.J. Reading (Derwent Valley Light Railway); A. Robinson; F. Robinson; H. Speed; N. Stanbra; E.A. Steel; H. Stones; B.D. Stoyel; E.S. Tonks; S.R. Wade; Mrs Welburn; G. Woodcock and W. Woolhouse.

My particular thanks are due to the late Miss A.G. Batty for first-hand information, and for the loan of a considerable number of rare photographs. But above all, my thanks must go to H.G.W. Household, who has most generously made available his extensive file, built up whilst preparing his account of the Sand Hutton for *The Locomotive.* This has been immense help, and has been the main basis for this book. Nor must I omit to mention Mr Household's excellent photographs with which he has been equally generous.

The locomotive, coach and wagon drawings have been prepared by Roy C. Link from maker's official drawings where available, and for his assistance I am deeply grateful, also to M. Swift for executing the maps and layout diagrams.

Sir Robert Walker, at the controls of SYNOLDA, taking Lady Synolda Walker and friends for a trip in the Hall grounds c. 1912-13. (Lady Walker is not identified.)

(K.E. Hartley collection)

The Estate's Daimler lorry, specially fitted for towing the fire engine, and carrying men and equipment.

(K.E. Hartley collection)

Introduction

Robert James Milo Walker, elder son of Sir James Heron Walker, the Third Baronet of Sand Hutton, Yorkshire, was born on March 18th, 1890.

He succeeded to the title and estate, and a very considerable fortune, at the age of ten, when Sir James died on November 25th, 1900. He studied at Trinity College, Cambridge, where he obtained his degree, and became an officer in the Coldstream Guards, ultimately rising to the rank of Major.

Known at one time as the richest man in the British Army, he always took the keenest interest in the affairs and welfare of his Regiment, and held fetes in the Hall grounds on its behalf. On these occasions his 15in gauge miniature railway carried many passengers, and collections were made by Miss Batty in aid of Association Funds. It has been said that no former Coldstream Guardsman was ever refused a job by Sir Robert.

In addition to the running of his estate, and operating a large and profitable retail coal business, the Fire Brigade Service was another matter of much importance to him, and the Sand Hutton Estate had its own fire-fighting men and equipment, which were developed to a high state of efficiency, and were responsible for the protection of a considerable area of the surrounding district.* Some little while before his untimely death, Sir Robert was presented with the Fire Brigade Medal for twenty years service, at a ceremony held in the Hall grounds.

Probably the chief of his numerous and varied activities, however, was a very great interest in railways. In the period 1895 to 1905—formative years in the life of the young Baronet—the railways of Britain were at probably the zenith of their prosperity, and the steam locomotive was held in admiration by all classes and ages. At this time too, the construction of miniature gauge railways was being undertaken by various wealthy gentlemen, partly for pleasure purposes, but also to serve the needs of their estates. In this connection, of course, the late Henry Greenly, and Bassett-Lowke Ltd, did a great deal to popularise the new development.

It was natural then, that Sir Robert should show a decided interest and become aware of such lines as that of the Duke of Westminster at Eaton Hall, near Chester; and no less, of the products of the famous Northampton firm. Whilst in his teens he had a large model railway lay-out attached to the iron railings surrounding the Hall grounds, and crossing the Drive by means of a swing bridge. By the time he was twenty-one, he had become greatly attracted by the possibilities of 15in gauge, and was making his early experiments preparatory to laying down his well-known Sand Hutton Miniature Railway—the line which ultimately became the nucleus of the subject of this booklet, the Sand Hutton Light Railway.

In addition to his own Sand Hutton line, Sir Robert Walker was also a director of the Derwent Valley Light Railway, and in various ways there was a cordial relationship between the two light railways. Further evidence of his keen and practical interest in local and national transport is found in the fact that Sir Robert was also a member of the Institute of Transport. His varied sporting activities included a love of cricket, and many fixtures were arranged and played at the Hall.

Sir Robert Walker died on February 11th, 1930, at the early age of 39, and was buried in the family vault in nearby Sand Hutton Churchyard. Had he lived until the 1960s as might quite reasonably have happened, there is no doubt in the writer's mind that the Sand Hutton Light Railway would still have been running, despite the loss of considerable traffic to road competition. Conversations with persons intimately connected with both the railway and Sir Robert amply support this view. Furthermore, in addition to Sir Robert's keenness, there are today many enthusiasts who would be only too glad to help in the preservation of a railway as unique as the Sand Hutton.

*The full history of the Estate Fire Brigade is not known but certainly Sir Robert had a Merryweather fire engine of traditional style by 1921. A second, very similar, engine by the same makers was obtained in 1924. These coal-fired engines were at first drawn by horses, but were soon adapted for haulage by a Daimler lorry, which had been fitted with seats, full driver's cab, and carried the men and extra equipment. A third, oil-fired, engine was acquired in about 1925. The Sand Hutton Brigade frequently took part in the Fire Drill Competitions against teams from York, Hull, Leeds, Harrogate, etc., and usually acquitted itself with credit.

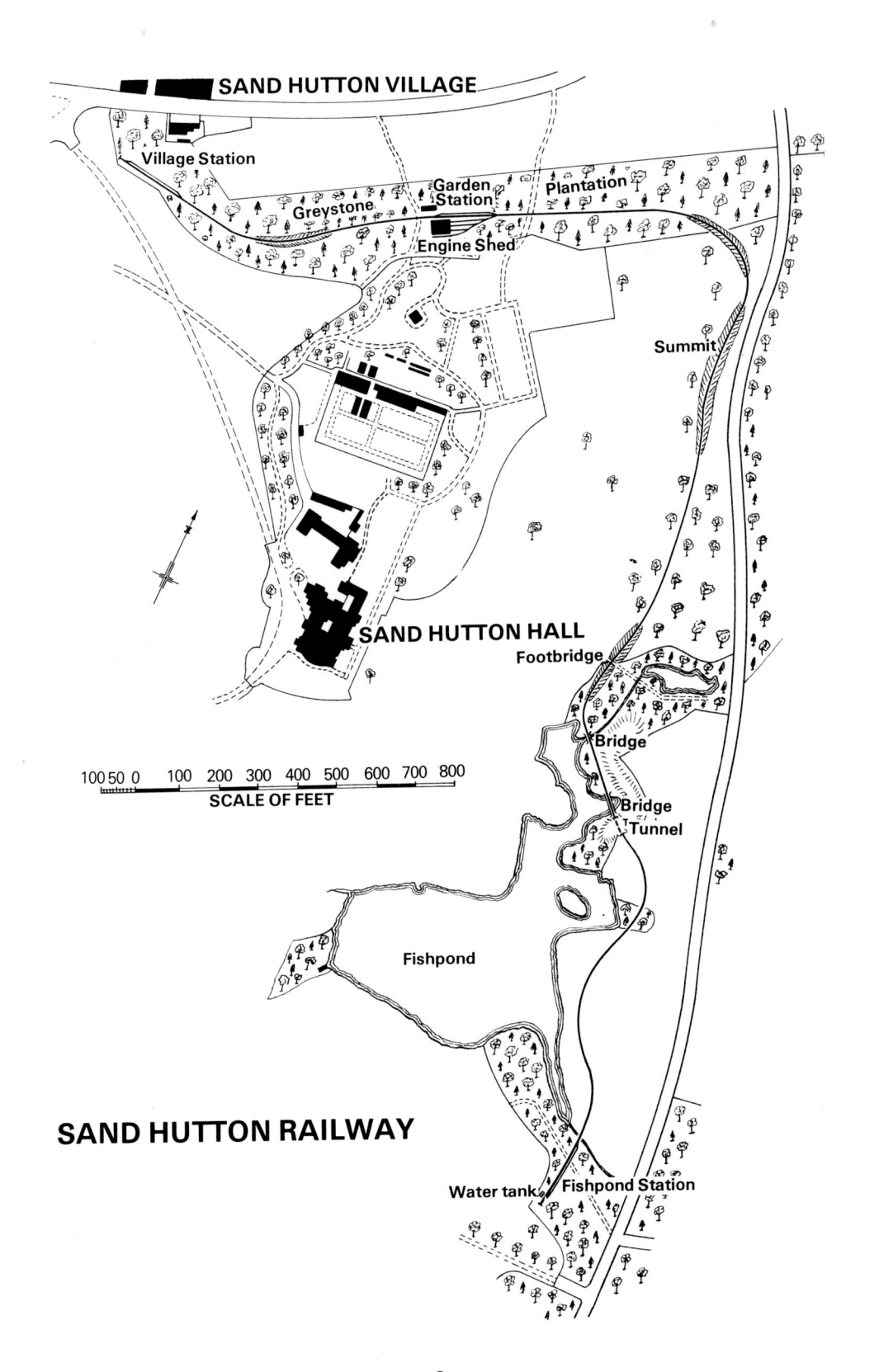

SAND HUTTON RAILWAY

SAND HUTTON VILLAGE

Village Station
Greystone
Garden Station
Plantation
Engine Shed
Summit
SAND HUTTON HALL
Footbridge
Bridge
Bridge
Tunnel
Fishpond
Water tank
Fishpond Station

100 50 0   100 200 300 400 500 600 700 800
SCALE OF FEET

Chapter 1

THE SAND HUTTON MINIATURE RAILWAY, 1912-1914

SYNOLDA and a passenger train crossing the bridge over part of the lake. (K.E. Hartley collection)

Sir Robert Walker stated in his article in the *Railway Magazine* for December 1924, that he commenced experiments with the 15in gauge in 1910. Unfortunately, no information as to the nature and extent of these early trials appears to be obtainable now, despite considerable enquiry. However, it seems that in the early part of 1912, he had decided to lay down a railway in the extensive grounds of Sand Hutton Hall. Situated in a delightful part of Yorkshire, the surroundings of the mansion afforded full scope for the installation of a really picturesque pleasure line, as will shortly be seen from the description of the route.

Towards the end of the year, 350 yards of track had been laid, and the new Bassett-Lowke Class 30 4-4-2 type locomotive SYNOLDA had been delivered. The exact date of the construction of the rest of the line is not known, but presumably this took place in 1913. At any rate, by the end of that year, the total length of the railway was 1,245 yards. The line was further extended by ¼ mile early in 1914, to the Cricket Field. It is understood that the intention was to continue a line right round the Hall, giving a total run of nearly two miles. Whether the commencement of World War I, in August 1914, had anything to do with the non-completion of this section is not known; but a likely answer is that Sir Robert already had thoughts on the far bigger scheme of reaching Warthill, and making the railway serve the needs of his estate, rather than running it purely for pleasure.

From the accompanying plan it will be seen that the railway commenced at a point about 50 yards inside the entrance to the main drive up to the Hall, and close to Sand Hutton village. Appropriately, this terminus was known as Village Station. There were no buildings here, but a platform and a run-round loop 43 yards long were provided.

At the start the line was level, but in the course of the 200 yards run to Garden Station, it soon began to fall, at gradients of 1 in 100, 1 in 120 and finally 1 in 90. Shortly before reaching this station—the main one on the railway—the track was carried on an embankment approximately 4ft high, and immediately before entering it, crossed a pathway to the Hall on the level. The first 450 yards of the line were laid through Greystone Plantation, a delightfully picturesque area of trees, and the views were very fine, particularly along the lengthy straight section which commenced at the station.

As its name implies, this was adjacent to the Hall gardens, and on the other side of the line the village school was not far away. The engine and carriage shed, a neat timber structure 37ft long and 12ft 9in wide was situated here, and accommodated all the rolling stock on three tracks. There was a fourth line alongside the shed. On the opposite side of the main running line was a timber built platform, 36ft long by 3ft wide, and beyond this was a 41 yard long loop.

A second asphalted path was crossed almost immediately beyond this point, which also marked the beginning of a bank 272 yards in length, and having a gradient of 1 in 100 at one part. About half-way up this bank the line emerged from the plantation on an embankment about 100 yards long and situated on a very severe curve, and then immediately afterwards entered a cutting of about 150 yards. This had a depth of from 4ft to 6ft, and was dug out of clay soil. The highest point on the railway was situated approximately half way along the cutting, 567 yards from Village Station and 104 feet above sea level.

There followed a continuous descent for the next 300 yards or so, much of it at 1 in 70 and 1 in 75, with slightly easier stretches of 1 in 100, and a final drop at 1 in 60 to the lakeside. This last section was on a fairly sharp curve and ran through a small plantation, where there was a 5ft 6in deep rock cutting spanned by a rustic bridge. Emerging from this cutting, the track crossed a small stream by means of a substantial timber bridge which had a span of 14ft 9in, and rested on stone abutments 3ft wide. The line was now alongside the lake, and very soon crossed a corner of it over a two-span timber bridge of 27ft 3in opening.

Immediately after this second bridge came the inevitable tunnel, 30ft long, through a small shrubbery, and constructed on the cut and cover method. For the remainder of its length the line followed the edge of the lake fairly closely, which resulted in a series of curves, some of them being severe. A second stream, just below the lake sluice, was crossed shortly before arriving at the terminus, Fishpond. Here was a large square water tank, on timber supports, for replenishing the tender tank, a timber-built platform, and a 45 yard long run round loop completed the layout. There was no station at the Cricket Field, and its exact position cannot now be discovered.

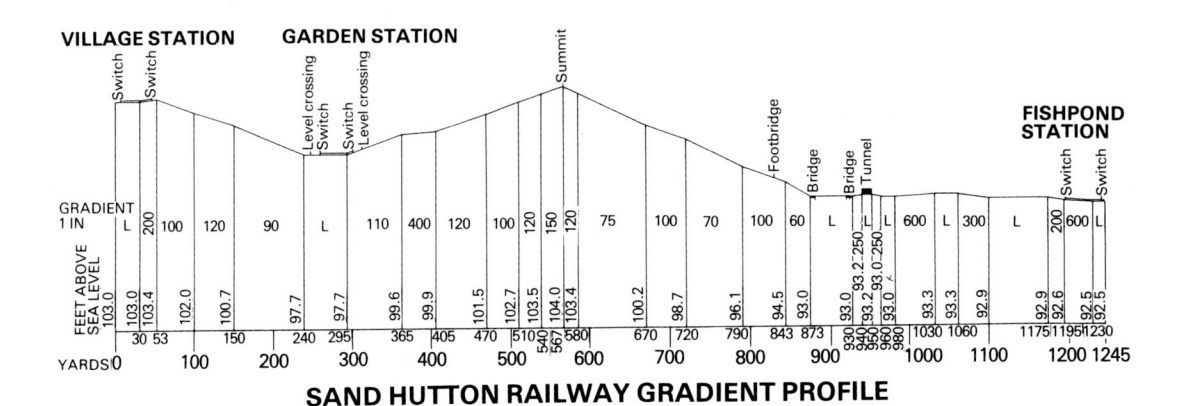

SAND HUTTON RAILWAY GRADIENT PROFILE

SYNOLDA, with a train of all the passenger vehicles, at Fishpond station c. 1912-13.
(K.E. Hartley collection)

    The track itself consisted of 16 lb per yard steel rail, in 23ft lengths, laid partly on standard gauge sleepers cut into three pieces each 3ft long, and partly on small-section (4in by 3in by 3ft long) sleepers cut on the estate. Eight of these latter, and seven of the former were used to each rail length. Two coach screws, with wrought iron clips, were used to secure the rail to each sleeper, and cinder ballast was employed, being packed to a depth of about 2in below the sleepers, and up to the top of them. The track was thus very substantial, and was laid on a formation 6ft wide in the case of embankments, and 4ft wide in the cuttings.

    The line became quite well known in the district, and picture postcards of it were to be bought locally at one time. Apart from the entertainment and pleasure afforded to Sir Robert and his numerous guests on private occasions the railway—no less than the Hall grounds—was frequently open to more public enjoyment, as on the occasion of garden parties and fetes. Needless to say, the children of Sand Hutton village were keenly interested in the little line, and it is said that the prospect of a ride on the railway after attending Sunday School was a big inducement to certain youngsters who would, no doubt, otherwise have endeavoured to forego their religious instruction!

    This, then was the Sand Hutton Miniature Railway in the days before the 1914 War.

Chapter 2
THE BASSETT-LOWKE 4-4-2 & SYNOLDA

Before describing the locomotive bought by Sir Robert Walker for use on his miniature railway, it may be of interest to refer to the earlier 4-4-2 type engines built by the famous Northampton firm of W.J. Bassett-Lowke Ltd., founded originally to manufacture models in gauges up to 3¼in. At the turn of the century miniature steam locomotives, invariably styled after the famous New York Central Railroad 4-4-0 No.999, began to appear on passenger-carrying railways of 9½in to 22in gauge in Amusement Parks across America. Four of these engines were imported into Britain, two being used by C.W. Bartholomew on his 15in gauge line connecting his residence with Blakesley station, on the Stratford-upon-Avon & Midland Junction Railway, in Northamptonshire.

It is probable that Bassett-Lowke saw an opportunity to emulate this development in Britain and, with Henry Greenly as his designer and engineer, he formed Miniature Railways (Great Britain) Ltd, in 1904. Late that year Greenly designed the first Bassett-Lowke 15in gauge locomotive—the legendary 4-4-2 LITTLE GIANT—which was completed at Northampton in May 1905. After trials on the Duke of Westminster's Eaton Hall line, near Chester, the new locomotive entered service on their initial operation at South Shore, Blackpool. LITTLE GIANT was built to a scale of 3in to 1ft, and was the prototype for Class 10, the most numerous of the three Atlantic classes, examples of which worked on a number of pleasure lines in England and Wales, as well as at Exhibitions in several European countries.

The Improved Little Giant (Class 20) first appeared in 1912. Although similar in appearance to its predecessor, it had a large boiler, larger wheels and cylinders, and was altogether a heavier and more powerful locomotive. Three examples were built; the first for King Rama VI of Siam in 1912, one for Southport in the same year, and the last for the Fairbourne Railway in 1914-15.

The final design of Atlantic produced at Northampton was Class 30, of which only three were built. It was a very handsome, new design, considerably larger and claimed to be 30% more powerful than the Class 20, and intended to handle a maximum load of 90 passengers. Known also as the SANS PAREIL class, it was offered in the firm's 1911 catalogue for £380, and had the following dimensions, from which it would appear to have been built to a somewhat larger scale than the earlier engines:

Length of engine & tender	16ft 9in*
Width overall	2ft 5in
Weight	2tons 5cwt*
Bogie wheel diameter	9½in
Coupled wheel diameter	1ft 8in
Trailing wheel diameter	11¼in
Cylinders—bore & stroke	4.1/8in × 6¾in*
Boiler—diameter & length	1ft 7in × 6ft 6in
Number of tubes	41
Boiler pressure	130 lb/sq in*

The first engine, No.30, was completed in 1912. Bearing the name of his (first) wife, SYNOLDA; this was the locomotive which Sir Robert Walker bought for his Sand Hutton Railway. The boiler was very large, and had a wide firebox giving a heating surface of 11,000 sq.in. A grid-iron pattern steam drier in the smokebox gave a moderate degree of superheat, and the cylinders were furnished with forced lubrication. The valves, on top of the cylinders, were actuated by Stephenson's valve gear with intermediate linkage, and an underslung basket grate allowed a moderately thick fire.

*SYNOLDA is described in *The Railway Magazine,* March 1914, as being 15ft 9in long, weighing 2 tons 12 cwt in working order, having cylinders 4in × 6¾in, and a boiler pressure of 120 lb/sq.in. The Bassett-Lowke catalogue of 1914 gives the boiler pressure as 130 lb/sq.in, and quotes a price for the Class 30 as £450 ex-works.

A test train of the entire passenger stock, loaded to capacity, in the Hall grounds, believed to be in 1913. (K.E. Hartley collection)

Cab fittings included a pull-out type regulator, water gauge, pressure gauge, two injectors, steam brake on the engine, blower control and vacuum gauge—for the coaches were equipped with a modified form of vacuum braking, with ejector on the locomotive.

The tender ran on two four-wheel bogies, and carried 55 galls. of water, in addition to a fair amount of coke for firing. The driver was accommodated on a full-width seat at the front end—it could, if need be, seat two persons side by side.

The locomotive and tender were highly finished in green, lined out in black and white, and with the initials S.H.R. in shaded gold characters on the tender sides. A coloured postcard issued by the Locomotive Publishing Co., circa 1913, shows both dome and safety valve cover to have been of polished brass, but the chimney was plain cast iron. SYNOLDA was a fine example of model engineering, and fully substantiated the maker's claim for it to be the most powerful 15in gauge locomotive so far built.

Some very interesting load and speed tests were recorded in *The Railway Magazine* for March, 1914, and by the courtesy of the Editor details of these are recorded here. It must be borne in mind that the nature of the original layout did not permit of continuous high speed running, owing to the numerous curves, but there is little doubt that SYNOLDA was capable of maximum speeds in the region of 35 miles an hour.

On Runs No. 1 and 2, the complete train—four open four-wheelers, the closed bogie saloon and the brake van—was in use, with a load of 44 passengers, and with the addition of a tip wagon loaded with 2½ tons of sand—a total load of 8 tons 4 cwt behind the tender. In relation to the weight of the locomotive and tender this was equivalent to 375 tons on the standard gauge. Nevertheless, the almost entirely uphill 300 yards stretch between the 300 and 600 yard posts were traversed in 46 and 44 seconds respectively—speeds of 13.3 and 14 m.p.h. In each case, the maximum speed was on a 100 yard downhill stretch, when 18.6 m.p.h. was obtained. Compared with the prototype, these results were certainly very good, bearing in mind the load.

On the third run, the ballast truck was detached, and there were but 3 passengers, the load being 2 tons 12 cwt — exactly equalling the weight of the engine and tender — say 120 tons on 4ft 8½in gauge. This light load presented no trouble at all, but the frequent slacks for the various curves rather spoilt the times. None the less, the first 400 yards were covered in just one minute — 200 yards were run in 21 seconds, or at the rate of 19.5 m.p.h. Another 100 yard section was traversed at 22.7 m.p.h.

For the fourth run, timed like the three previous ones by stop-watch, the load was reduced to one four-wheeler and the bogie coach, with 3 passengers — 19cwt — and a maximum speed of 23.25 m.p.h. was recorded — just about the safe limit on this curving lay-out.

The return runs were made with the engine propelling the train, and this accounts for the slower time on Run No. 5 — with seven assorted vehicles in front of the engine, some caution was necessary. On Run No. 6, with a load of 2 tons 12 cwt the average speed up the 1 in 75 stretch between posts 700 and 600 was 15.7 m.p.h. This, however, was surpassed on Run 7, when with the 19 cwt load, the maintained speed right up the 1 in 70 and 1 in 75 from post 800 to post 600 was 18.6 m.p.h.

The fastest run of the day was made in the same direction as these three trips, running tender first, and with the 19 cwt load. The curve between posts 500 and 400 was taken faster than usual, and then the regulator was slammed wide open. A stop-watch reading was not possible, but observers at Garden Station reckoned the speed to be fully 30 m.p.h., and certainly SYNOLDA was quite capable of such a speed.

Full details of these runs appear in the table below:

	Down (Engine Pulling Load)					Up (Engine Pushing Load)		
Run No.	1	2	3	4	Run No.	5	6	7
Load	8T.4C	8T.4C	2T.12C	0T.19C	Load	8T.4C	2T.12C	0T.19C
Yards	M.S.	M.S.	M.S.	M.S.	Yards	M.S.	M.S.	M.S.
0	0-0	0-00	0-00	0-00	1245	0-00	0-00	0-00
100	0-20	0-23	0-26	0-25	1200	0-22	0-10	0-12
200	0-35	0-41	0-39	0-37	1100	0-55	0-28	0-32
300	0-50	0-54	0-50	0-47	1000	1-16	0-43	0-43
400	1-04	1-09	1-00*	0-56*	900	1-35	0-54*	0-54*
500	1-20	1-21	1-14	1-07	800	1-53	1-07	1-07
600	1-36	1-38	1-27	1-17	700	2-15	1-19	1-17
700	1-49	1-52	1-36	1-26	600	2-40	1-32	1-28
800	2-00*	2-03*	1-47*	1-37*	500	3-03	1-45*	1-39*
900	2-15	2-16	2-01	1-50	400	3-16	1-56	1-50
1000	2-30	2-33	2-14*	2-03	300	3-30	2-05	1-59
1100	2-44	2-47	2-27	2-16	200	4-04	2-14	2-09
1200	3-03	3-04	2-41	2-30	100	4-58	2-25	2-30
1245	3-15	3-16	2-51	2-40	0	5-20	2-53	2-44
Average Speed MPH	13-1	13-2	14-9	15-9		8-0	14-7	15-5

*Speed eased for curves

Two further Class 30 engines were built. No. 31 left Northampton in 1913 for Geneva, and worked here and at the 1914 Exhibition in Oslo before being returned to Ravenglass in 1915 to become the first 15in gauge locomotive on the Ravenglass & Eskdale Railway. No. 32, the final example, was not completed until 1924 although the frames and castings had been ready in 1914. It was ordered by Count Louis Zborowski for his Highams Railway, Canterbury, but the Count died in a crash before he could take delivery, and COUNT LOUIS, as the locomotive was named, went to the Fairbourne Railway in 1925, where it remains to this day.

Chapter 3
15IN. GAUGE ROLLING STOCK

The first rolling stock on the miniature railway consisted of four of Bassett-Lowke's standard 4-wheel open coaches, each seating eight persons, in two compartments. By courtesy of the makers, the detailed specification of these vehicles, taken from their 1914 catalogue of 15in Garden Railways Equipment, is now quoted:

"The Bodies are made up from best well-seasoned Burmese teak with a good figure and grain. The Sides are framed up in heavy stuff and panelled up in best style with teak matching. Cast iron Steps are fitted to each entrance. The Bodies are fixed to the Underframe with Iron knees and can be easily removed for transport and repairs. The Underframes are constructed of the best English oak on the most approved lines. They are stiffened with steel longitudinal and cross stays and steel headstock bolts with forged palm pieces.

"A special design of combined Central Buffer and Coupling is fitted. This is made of steel throughout and of very substantial design, well calculated to stand rough and continual use. The Buffing and Draw springs are contained in one Cast-iron Cradle firmly bolted to the Underframe, and with steel Rubbing Plates fitted to the Headstock to take the blow when shunting. This Cradle is so designed that the pull comes on the Underframe longitudinally and not on the Headstock alone. Cast iron Axle Guards are fitted with a special pocket to carry the Riding Springs and protect them from mud, wet and other damage. The Axle Boxes are of a special type, cast in close-grained iron, with self-oiling Rings, and large oil wells so arranged as to run for months without attention. Large Inspection Doors are fitted to these so that the Oil Wells can be easily cleaned and the Axle examined without removing the Axle Box from the Hornplates. The Wheels are best quality Steel Alloy, shrunk on Steel Axles and truly turned on the treads and the flanges after shrinking on the Axles.

"The Coaches are finished in the best quality out-door varnish and lined with gold and blue lines. Underframes are painted best black enamel over the best lead paint. All iron-work black and the floor inside best grey paint. This style of finish looks particularly handsome, and requires less upkeep than any other style. They can be lettered to order in gold shaded letters, or if preferred, with solid brass letters. This latter is a very pleasing and durable style of lettering for out-door work."

From examination of a number of photographs, it seems that the coaches were not, in fact, lettered; nor were the striped awnings and teak-framed glass windscreens—which were optional extras—fitted on the Sand Hutton coaches. The length over headstocks was 8ft 2in, the wheel base 5ft 8in with wheels of 10½in diameter, and the weight empty was 7 cwt.

These coaches were equipped with a modified form of continuous vacuum brake in which the vacuum cylinder consisted of a spherical casting. This contained a rubber diaphragm connected direct to the brake levers. On the creation of a vacuum by the ejector on the locomotive, the diaphragm was sucked inwards and the brakes were applied. It will be noticed that, unlike the ordinary standard gauge vacuum brake, with this apparatus the vacuum was only created at the moment of applying the brakes. The vacuum pipes were set in a diagonal position on the ends of the rolling stock, in order to obtain sufficient flexibility in the connections. The 1914 price for the desirable extra was £14.10s.0d. (£14.50) per 4-wheel coach, which itself cost £52.10s.0d. (£52.50) or, for a "Second Quality" vehicle, £28.10s.0d. (£28.50).

In addition to the four Bassett-Lowke open 4-wheelers, there were two vehicles built at Sand Hutton by Sir Robert Walker. One was a bogie saloon coach which accommodated ten passengers on reversible garden seats, and had a centre corridor. It had two sliding doors; windows in each end in addition to those in the sides, and was quite a handsome and airy-looking vehicle, with none of the heavy and ungainly appearance of other 15in gauge closed coaches of the period. Presumably the bogies were of Bassett-Lowke manufacture. These, to quote their catalogue once more, had "four 8in diameter Steel Alloy Wheels, running in Padded Axle Boxes, Wheel centres, 24in, finished and painted flat colour. Price £8.8s.0d. (£8.40) each." The weight of this coach was 10 cwt, and the finish was in varnished teak, uniform with the other carriages.

Members of a local cycling club enjoying a trip over the Sand Hutton Railway on 18th April 1914. The location is at, or near, the Hall cricket field. (K.E. Hartley collection)

The other vehicle was a 4-wheel, covered passenger brake van, equipped with sliding doors—one on each side. The construction of this van was much more in the "Heywood" tradition. Unlike the saloon coach, there was no curvature to the sides; these and the ends were of horizontal match-boarding. The roof was lower than that on the coach, and had very little camber. An unusual feature was the provision of a couple of loco-type round look-out glasses in each end. There were benches at each end which seated a total of four persons. Like the bogie saloon, it weighed 10 cwt, and had the same teak finish. It is recorded that on one occasion, when a total load of 75 passengers was packed on to the train, no less than 17 of them were squeezed into this van!

There was also in 1913-14 a small 4-wheeled tip wagon, of which no details are now obtainable. Nor can anything be discovered about the additional stock which, it seems, must have been required for the construction and operation of the extensions to Warthill and Claxton in 1920.

As to the disposal of the 15in gauge stock only one thing seems to be certain. That is that the saloon coach did undoubtedly go to the Ravenglass & Eskdale Railway. This has been confirmed by Mr. Jones, and also by Mr. Peter le Neve-Foster, who was well acquainted with the Eskdale line for many years. There is photographic evidence in a view showing the 4 h.p. Douglas Scooter at Irton Road on a short winter train; the Sand Hutton vehicle is coupled next to the engine. On the R. & E.R. it was called "The Glass Coach", and was generally used on the morning train, and also on the Thursday market train. The guard in those days, an old coachman, used to smoke a rank old pipe in this carriage—to the intense annoyance of some of the ladies riding in it! The Glass Coach remained on the Eskdale Line until about 1928, and eventually ended its days as a green house in a neighbouring garden.

The fate of the van is a mystery, but it seems likely that the four open Bassett-Lowke coaches ended their working life at Ravenglass, although definite confirmation of this cannot be obtained.

Chapter 4: 15IN. GAUGE LINE; 1914-1920

The outbreak of the 1914-18 War quickly changed things around Sand Hutton. Sir Robert Walker had always been keen for his male employees to join the Territorials, and thus it came about that the village was soon without many of its menfolk. The Hall was more or less closed-down, and the railway and SYNOLDA entered upon a five-year spell of inactivity.

Sir Robert, accompanied by Lady Walker, was sent out to New Zealand, early in 1915, to help in the training of troops. He was joined soon afterwards by Mr. George L. Batty, the Estate engineer, who drove him about the country on his duties.

It was not until 1919 that they all returned to the United Kingdom. Sir Robert lost little time in re-organising affairs at Sand Hutton, and during the summer of that year, he had definitely decided to lay down a light railway to serve a part of the Estate.

The intention was to retain the 15in gauge, already in use, and on many occasions both Sir Robert and Mr. Batty worked late into the night, settling all the details. The necessary plans were eventually drawn up for the construction of a line from Warthill Station, on the York—Market Weighton line of the old North Eastern Rly; to the village of Scrayingham, on the eastern bank of the River Derwent, passing en route through Sand Hutton and the neighbouring village of Bossall, with branch lines to Claxton and Barnby House—a total distance of 7¼ miles.

Application was made to the Light Railway Commissioners—at that time the responsible body—for the necessary Light Railway Order in November, 1919, and the Minister of Transport at that time, Sir Eric Geddes, gave the scheme his full support.

The following extract from the *N.E.R. Magazine* of the latter part of 1920, is quoted:

"The report of the proceedings of the Light Railways Commissioners during 1919 (Published June, 1920, price 2d. net) records the Commissioners approval of two new projects in the North of England, viz; the Sand Hutton Light Railway (Warthill to Claxton, Bossall and Scrayingham) and the South Shields Corporation Light Railway (South Shields to Cleadon).

"Regarding the Warthill scheme the report says: We may mention an application made last November for a narrow-gauge line from Warthill Station on the York and Market Weighton branch of the North Eastern Railway, near York, passing through the Sand Hutton Estate and crossing the River Derwent to Scrayingham, a distance of 5¼ miles (with branch lines of two miles to outlying farms); the scheme provides for passengers as well as for goods, and was brought forward, and will be financed, by Sir Robert Walker, Bart; and the Trustees of the property.

"We have settled an Order for submission to the Ministry of Transport, and hope the line may serve to show that agricultural light railways in any district which admits of, and obtains, a fully productive cultivation can be made and worked so economically as to be directly self-supporting, apart from the benefits which directly and indirectly accrue to the districts served."

The Order was granted in January, 1920, and confirmed by the Ministry of Transport on May 1st of that year.

Before examining the Order in more detail, however, it may be convenient to conclude the history of the railway in 15in gauge form. Work commenced on the first section, in May 1920, at the Warthill end, and some of the metals of the existing line were laid down. Good progress was made, and by the end of the year, the 15in main line was completed as far as Sand Hutton, and the construction of the Claxton branch had got as far as the brickworks—a length of line totalling about 3 miles. As will be seen from the gradient profile of the S.H.L.R., these parts of the line were comparatively level, and the miniature 4-4-2 locomotive experienced no particular difficulty in working the ballast forward. However, the experience gained in building and operating these sections of the line, and the knowledge that onwards from Sand Hutton very undulating country, and consequently heavy gradients, would be encountered, made it evident that to deal with heavy loads, something bigger than 15in gauge, and "scale model" locomotives, would be required.

Sir Robert was no doubt fully aware of the rugged and powerful Heywood engines used at Duffield Bank, and Eaton, but there seems to be no evidence that he contemplated using this style of motive power at Sand Hutton. In any case, these engines had already gone to the Ravenglass & Eskdale Rly., and Bassett-Lowke had virtually ceased production of 15in gauge locos, in 1914. We do not know, in fact, what type of engine Sir Robert had in mind, but back in July 1916, *Models, Railways and Locomotives,* had contained descriptions and diagrams for a number of possible locomotives, which perhaps might provide a clue.

All four designs were for approximately one-third full size, but they bore little resemblance to the Bassett-Lowke,

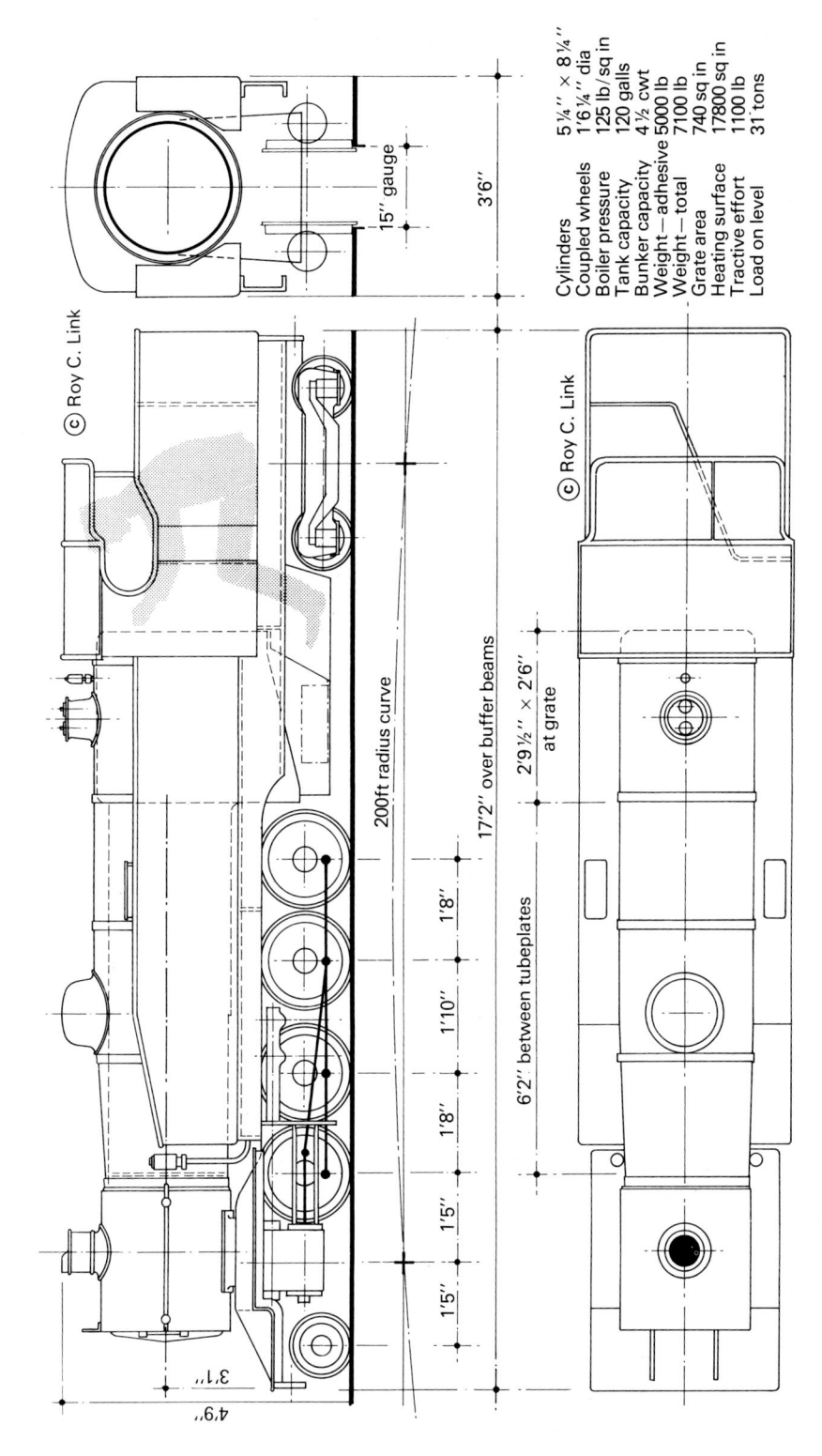

PROPOSED 2-8-4 TYPE ARTICULATED LOCO. 15IN GAUGE (from Jubb Ltd, Sheffield, drawing No. ML 20)

Cylinders	5¼" × 8¼"
Coupled wheels	1'6¼" dia
Boiler pressure	125 lb/sq in
Tank capacity	120 galls
Bunker capacity	4½ cwt
Weight — adhesive	5000 lb
Weight — total	7100 lb
Grate area	740 sq in
Heating surface	17800 sq in
Tractive effort	1100 lb
Load on level	31 tons

© Roy C. Link

or Heywood engines, being more akin to some 3ft 6in gauge machines built for service overseas. The first type was a typically British 0-6-0 goods loco, though the other proposals were for articulated designs. One was a variation of the Garratt principle, the other two were based on the single-boiler Fairlie. It seems unlikely that any of these were ever built, but there was a further development of the single-boiler Fairlie principle, of which a more detailed drawing was discovered by Mr. K. Hoole, in the course of his research into the British Railways archives at York about 1968, and I am indebted to him for obtaining a copy of this and two other drawings from this source. Drawing No. ML20 carries the name Jubb Ltd., Sheffield, and shows "A Proposed 2-8-4 Type Articulated Loco" for 15in gauge. It is dated Oct. 30, 1919 and signed Henry Greenly. A further drawing, ML21, is of a "15in Gauge Open Bogie Wagon", signed by Mr. Greenly; and a third drawing—not numbered, but titled "Proposed 15in gauge Open Bogie Wagon"—is of a vehicle having hinged drop sides, in three sections. The date of these drawings immediately suggests that the locomotive and wagons could be for the extensions in mind for the Sand Hutton 15in gauge railway, but unfortunately there is no indication of this on the prints. However, the fact that the drawings were originally with the N.E.R. at York backs up the suggestion that the proposals were for Sand Hutton, though it is now doubtful if the truth will ever be known.

SYNOLDA was capable of working the more or less level lines to Warthill and Claxton, though brick and coal trains on the latter section would sooner or later have required an engine of greater power. Beyond Sand Hutton, however, the terrain was undulating and ultimately involved gradients of 1 in 80, and even one of 1 in 65. Although the proposed 2-8-4 was to be a fairly large and powerful machine it was hardly in the same class as RIVER ESK of 1923 or the R.H. & D.R. Pacifics. It was, however, a great advance on former Bassett-Lowke designs, with outside cylinders and piston valves apparently worked by Greenly valve gear. The side tanks were cut away at the front end, this detail and the chimney being very characteristic of London & South Western Railway locomotives of the same period, when R.W. Urie was in charge. A table of dimensions appears on the drawing, and also the outline of a 200ft. radius curve—again suggesting Sand Hutton. The general proportions are much larger than previous designs, and in fact approximate more closely to one third scale of later 15in gauge locomotives.

The bogie wagon shown on drawing ML21 is also substantially designed with a heavy steel frame, modern bogies and vacuum brakes. If the design has any fault it is the small doors which could have been difficult to load and unload. This might be the reason for the alternative proposal drawing, obviously prepared by a junior draughtsman, perhaps at the N.E.R. carriage and wagon works at York. The overall dimensions are very similar to the Greenly design, but there are three large drop doors on each side with pin-and-wedge catches so familiar on main line wagons even today.

The firm of Jubb Ltd., will no doubt be unfamiliar to enthusiasts today, but before 1914, W.H. Jubb, a Sheffield man who owned an engineering works, was a well known model railway enthusiast. Steam driven locomotives in 1¾in, 2in and 2½in gauges were popular, and gauge 0 was the smallest standard size until the introduction of 00 late in 1922. About 1920 Jubb put a range of gauge 0 and gauge 1 steam locomotives and wooden bodied rolling stock on the market. The cheapest was a freelance four wheel tank locomotive with outside cylinders but more ambitious types were reasonably good models of main line prototypes. The firm's catalogue, like the models, was comparatively expensive, certainly for a lad still at school.

However, Jubb was well known to both Henry Greenly and Proctor Mitchell of the R. & E.R., and operated the 2in gauge Greystones Railway, which had complete signal interlocking and for which he built a number of locomotives. Bassett-Lowke built no more 15in gauge locomotives after 1914, with the exception of the class 30 4-4-2 COUNT LOUIS in 1925 for which parts were already on hand. Jubb Ltd. was therefore well placed in 1919 to enter the miniature locomotive construction business. In 1922 they built a 7¼in gauge 0-4-2 tank for the Saltwood Railway which is, I believe, still running though converted to an Atlantic. This was their largest locomotive so far as I can discover. The model railway equipment could not successfully compete with the established Northampton firm's products, and went off the market in the late 1920's.

I have never seen any other reference to this 2-8-4 design, which perhaps was never fully completed in detail. The authors of recent books on 15in gauge railways or locomotives make no mention of it, and George Woodcock, despite his long interest in miniature locomotives has been unable to throw any light on Greenly's proposal. Whilst it is interesting to speculate on how things might have turned out on the Sand Hutton, at the critical moment, December 1920, the 18in gauge 0-4-0 well tanks and rolling stock from Deptford Meat Depot became available, most likely at bargain prices. Sir Robert decided to change the gauge to 18in and use the more powerful Hunslet locomotives, thus effectively putting an end to any further developments on the smaller gauge. Work on the conversion started in 1921, and progressed steadily until finally the only stretch of 15in gauge track left was the 20 or 30 yards which included the tunnel. When the final item of rolling stock, the locomotive, SYNOLDA, was sold in 1922, the 15in gauge era ended.

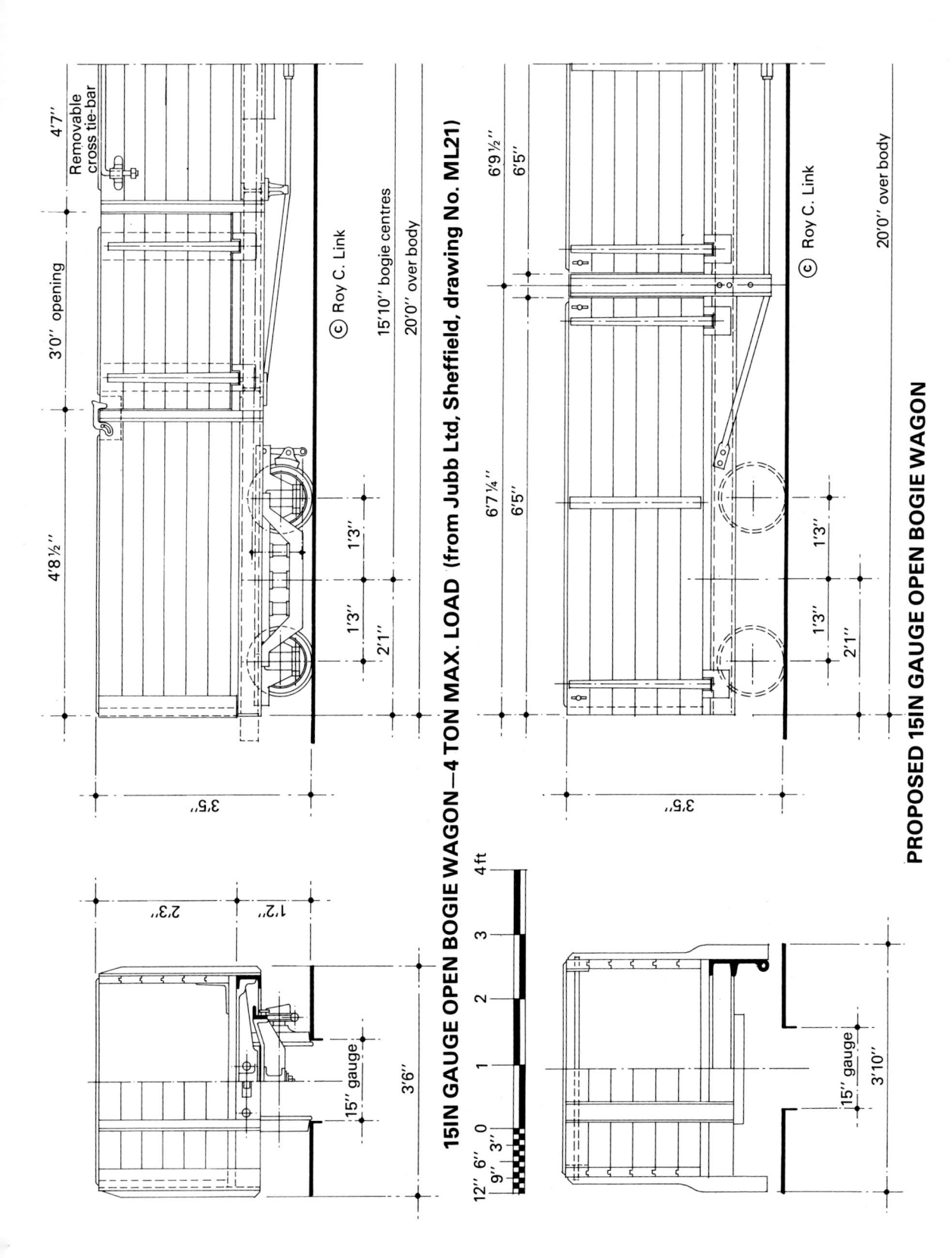

15IN GAUGE OPEN BOGIE WAGON—4 TON MAX. LOAD (from Jubb Ltd, Sheffield, drawing No. ML21)

PROPOSED 15IN GAUGE OPEN BOGIE WAGON

Chapter 5: THE LIGHT RAILWAY ORDER

As briefly mentioned in the previous chapter, the Light Railway Order—made under the Light Railway Acts of 1896 and 1912—incorporating the Company and authorising the construction of the Railway contained much of interest within its 23 pages. It is not, perhaps, desirable to quote this publication in full, but the more interesting provisions are set out in some detail, as they contain much information which has not hitherto been published.

The Preamble to the Order states that the Application was made in November, 1919, and that the Order should come into force on the date on which it should be confirmed by the Ministry of Transport. The early sections deal with the title of the railway, etc., and

Sec. 4   "Incorporation of the Company", states that "Sir Robert James Milo Walker, Bart, and Edward Arthur Field Whittle Herbert and Henry Angus Watson and all other persons and corporations who have already subscribed to or shall hereafter become proprietors in the undertaking...are hereby united into a Company for the making and maintaining of the Railway."

Sec. 11   gives very precise details, and empowered the Company "to make and maintain Railways, Sidings, Junctions, Turntables, Bridges, Culverts, Drains, Viaducts, Tunnels, Stations, Approaches, Roads, Yards, Buildings and other works and conveniences connected therewith." The said Railways were:
"A Railway (No. 1) 5 miles 2 furlongs 8 chains or thereabouts in length situated in the parishes of Stockton-on-the-Forest of Warthill Freehold (Detached No. 1) of Warthill Copyhold (Detached No. 1) of the Sand Hutton and of Butter Crambe with Bossall in the Rural District of Flaxton in the North Riding of the County of York and in the parish of Scrayingham in the Rural District of Pocklington in the East Riding of the County of York commencing at a point on the south side of and adjacent to the public road passing Warthill Station about 165 yards north-east of the level crossing at that Station proceeding thence in an easterly direction for about 3 furlongs crossing the road from Stockton-on-the-Forest to Warthill and there entering and thence passing in a north-easterly direction for about 1 mile along and upon the road and bridleway known as the Warthill—Sand Hutton Lane, thence generally in a north-easterly and easterly direction for about 3 miles crossing the River Derwent and terminating at a point adjacent to and on the north-west side of the road leading from Butter Crambe to Scrayingham about 45 yards south of Glebe Farm Scrayingham: Provided that Railway (No. 1) between points shown on the Plan as being 2½ and 3 furlongs respectively from the commencement of the said Railway shall be constructed and maintained on an alignment shown on a plan the 26th day of January, 1920, signed by J. TRIFFITT and deposited with the Ministry of Transport.
"A Railway (No. 2) 1 mile 3 furlongs 6 chains or thereabouts in length situated in the parishes of Sand Hutton and of Claxton in the said Rural District of Flaxton commencing in the said Warthill—Sand Hutton Lane by a junction with Railway (No. 1) at a point on that Railway about 560 yards south of Gravel Pit Farm and 400 yards east of White Sike Farm passing along and upon the said Lane crossing the road from York to Sand Hutton and terminating at a point on the east side of Ings Lane at its point of intersection with Whinney Lane.
"A Railway (No. 3) 3 furlongs 5 chains or thereabouts in length wholly situated in the parish of Butter Crambe with Bossall in the said Rural District of Flaxton commencing by a junction with Railway (no. 1 at a point on that Railway about 430 yards south-east of Bossall Church and about 580 yards south-west of Barnby House and terminating at a point where the occupation road enters the stackyard of the said Barnby House."

Sec. 12   **Gauge of Railway and Motive Power.**
The railway shall be constructed on a gauge of 15in or such other gauge not exceeding 2ft 0in as the Company may determine and the motive power shall be steam or such other motive power as the Ministry of Transport may approve: Provided that nothing in this Order shall authorise the Company to use electrical power as motive power on the railway.

Sec. 21   Powers to deviate from the Plan and the Section, both (1) laterally and (2) vertically were granted, subject to certain conditions. The radius (3) of any curve could be altered provided that it was not reduced below 2 chains, and gradients also could be altered, so long as they became no steeper than 1 in 25.

Sec. 24   **Level Crossings without Gates**
With respect to every level crossing of a public carriage road the following provisions shall apply:
(a) Where the railway or the road is fenced such cattleguards or other suitable contrivances shall be constructed at the side of the road and so maintained as to prevent cattle or horses on the road from entering upon the Railway.

(b) At each of two points one 200 yards along the Railway in one direction from the level crossing and other 200 yards along the Railway in the other direction from the level crossing there shall be erected and maintained a white post standing 5ft above ground and bearing upon it and so as to plainly legible by the driver of an engine approaching the level crossing a figure indicating the number of miles per hour which is fixed under the provisions of this Order as the maximum rate of speed of a train or engine approaching and within a distance of 200 yards from the level crossing.

(c) At each of two points one fifty yards or thereabouts along the road in one direction from the point of crossing and the other fifty yards or thereabouts along the road in the other direction from the point of crossing there shall be erected and maintained by the Company a noticeboard cautioning the public to beware of the trains.

Sec. 27 Fences
The Company are not bound to fence the Railway provided that cattle guards, etc., were constructed and maintained where the Railway crossed existing fences and where any fences constructed between the Railway and such land came to an end.

Sec. 29 Bridge over the River Derwent
"...(3) The Company shall carry the Railway over the River Derwent and the towing path thereof by means of a bridge with a single span and no part of the underside of such bridge shall be lower than fifteen feet above the summer level of the river at the point of crossing...

"...(6) The bridge to be completed within one year from the date at which it is commenced. At all times during construction and subsequent repair the Company to leave open and uninterrupted a navigable waterway of sufficient width, depth and headway to conveniently accommodate vessels using the river, with a tow path of not less than 4ft in width, at all times free from obstruction."

Sec. 31 Opening for Passenger Traffic
(1) No part of the Railway shall be opened for the public conveyance of passengers until one month after notice in writing of such intention has been given by the Company to the Minister of Transport of the time when the Company considers the line to be sufficiently completed for safe conveyance of passengers and ready for inspection.

(2) If any part of the Railway is so opened by the Company without such notice the Company shall forfeit to His Majesty the sum of £20 for every day during which it continues open until such notices have been duly given and shall have expired.

Sec. 34 Power to enter into agreements with N.E.R. Co.
The Company...and the N.E.R. may, subject to certain provisions, enter into agreements for the Construction, Maintenance and Management of the Railway; the use or working of the Railway, and conveyance of traffic thereon; the fixing of rates, charges, tolls, etc, in respect of traffic; the supply and maintenance of Rolling Stock, etc., and the employment of officers and servants for conducting traffic and all other matters.

Sec. 37 states that if mechanical power other than steam is used on the Railway such power shall not be used without consent of, and subject to penalties and conditions imposed by the Minister of Transport.

Sec. 38 The Company was entitled to demand tolls for the use of the Railway by "any other person with carriages and engines".

Sec. 39 Rates for Merchandise
Subject to certain provisions, the classification of merchandise traffic including perishable goods and the schedule of maximum rates and charges applicable thereto and the regulations and provisions of the Railway Rates and Charges No. 15 (N.E.R. etc.) Order Confirmation Act 1892 shall be applicable and apply to the Company.

Sec. 40 Charges for small parcels.
For the conveyance...of small parcels not exceeding 500 lb. in weight, the Company may demand and take any charges not exceeding the following:

For any parcel not exceeding 7 lb. in weight	— Sixpence
For any parcel not over 7 lb. but under 14 lb.	— Ninepence
For any parcel not over 14 lb. but under 28 lb.	— One Shilling
For any parcel not over 28 lb. but under 56 lb.	— One Shilling and Threepence

For any parcel exceeding 56 lb. but not exceeding 500 lb. in weight, the Company may demand any sum they think fit.

Sec. 41 Maximum Rates for Passengers
Subject to the provisions of the Order, the maximum rate of charge...for the conveyance of passengers...shall not exceed:

For every passenger conveyed in 1st Class carriage   4½d per mile
For every passenger conveyed in 2nd Class carriage   3d per mile
For every passenger conveyed in 3rd Class carriage   1½d per mile
For every passenger conveyed...for a less distance than 3 miles, the Company may charge as for 3 miles, and every fraction of a mile beyond 3 miles or any greater number of miles shall be deemed a mile.

Sec. 42 The "free" allowances for Passengers Luggage were laid down as:
1st Class passengers, 120 lb.
2nd Class passengers, 100 lb., and 3rd Class 60 lb.

Sec. 43 **Special Trains Charges.**
The restrictions as to the charges to be made for passengers shall not extend to any special train run upon the Railway in respect of which the Company may make any such charges as they think fit but shall apply only to the ordinary trains appointed by the Company for the conveyance of passengers upon the Railway.

Sec. 44 **Capital**
The capital of the Company shall be £25,000 in 2,500 shares of £10 each.

Sec. 48 The Company was authorised to borrow on mortgage of the undertaking in respect of their capital of £25,000 any sum or sums not exceeding in the whole £8,000.

Sec. 58 "The provisions of the First Schedule to this Order shall be observed if required by the Minister of Transport."

The First Schedule (Quoted in full)
"**Permanent Way** The rails used shall weigh not less than 16 pounds per yard or 20 pounds per yard where the Minister of Transport may so require.
"On curves with radii of less than 3 chains a check-rail shall be provided. If flat-bottomed rails and wooden sleepers are used—
(a) The rails at the joints shall be secured to the sleepers by fang or other through bolts or by coach-screws or by double spikes on the outside of the rail with a bearing plate; and
(b) The rails on curves with radii of less than three chains shall be secured on the outside of the outer rail to each sleeper by a fang or other through bolt or by a coachscrew or by double spikes with a bearing plate; and
(c) The rails on curves with radii of less than three chains shall be tied to gauge by iron or steel ties at suitable intervals or in such other manner as may be approved by the Minister of Transport.
"**Turntables** No turntables need be provided.
"**Electrical Communication** If the Minister of Transport requires means of electrical communication to be provided on the line the Company shall make that provision in such manner as the M.O.T. may direct.
"**Signals** At places where under the system of working for the time being in force trains may cross or pass one another there shall be a home-signal for each direction at or near the entrance points. If the home-signal cannot be seen from a distance of a quarter of a mile a distant-signal must be erected at that distance at least from the entrance points. The home-signals and distant-signals may be worked from the station by wires or otherwise.
"Every signal-arm shall be weighted as to fly to and remain at danger on the breaking at any point of the connection between the arm and the lever working it.
"Precautions shall be taken to the satisfaction of the M.O.T. to ensure that no signal can be lowered unless the points are in the proper position and that two conflicting signals cannot be lowered simultaneously.
"**Platforms, etc.** Platforms shall be provided to the satisfaction of the M.O.T. unless all carriages in use on the Railway for the conveyance of passengers are constructed with proper and convenient means of access to and from the same from and to the level of the ground on the outside of the rail.
"There shall be no obligation on the Company to provide shelter or conveniences at any station or stopping-place."

The Second Schedule.
Describes Properties of which portions only may be taken, e.g. "Scrayingham, No. 4 on Deposited Plan, Stackyard and Fowl House."
The foregoing Order is hereby confirmed by the Minister of Transport. Given under the Seal of the Minister of Transport this first day of May, One thousand nine hundred and twenty.

ERNEST G. MOGGRIDGE,
Assistant Secretary."

Chapter 6

THE SAND HUTTON LIGHT RAILWAY

*No 12 in the woods near Sand Hutton.
(K.E. Hartley collection)*

Progress with the conversion of gauge, and further extension of the main line, was such that by April, 1922, it was possible to open the new 18in railway for goods traffic right through from Warthill to Kissthorn's Sidings, and at the same time, the whole of the Claxton branch was also in operation — at total of just over 4½ miles.

Labour costs in the early 1920's were prohibitively high compared with pre-1914 standards — in point of fact they were about double — and Sir Robert found himself forced to abandon any further new construction until the following year, 1923, when in May work commenced on the main line. By December, the railway was completed and open for traffic as far as Bossall, and the steeply-graded branch line to Barnby House was also in use. Thus there remained only the ½ mile to Scrayingham to complete the S.H.L.R. as authorised. But this last portion contained what would without doubt have been the major engineering feature of the railway — the 100ft single span bridge over the River Derwent. While the construction of the rest of the line was well within the scope of the local labour force, this bridge was a different matter altogether. The cost was estimated at £1,000, and this meant that the final ½ mile would have been a fairly expensive piece of line. Whether traffic from the Scrayingham area would ever have warranted this expense now seems very doubtful. It would appear that the Directors of the S.H.L.R. eventually reached the same conclusion, for the Scrayingham section was never completed, the only portion actually built being a short length of track beyond the junction of the Barnby House branch.

The cost of construction of the Sand Hutton Light Railway was approximately £4,400 per mile, and Sir Robert expressed the opinion *(The Railway Magazine* May, 1924) that pre-1914 the figure would probably have been nearer £2,000 per mile. In his article he gave some interesting arguments in favour of the true narrow gauge (i.e. around 2ft 0in gauge) and these were supported by the table reproduced herewith giving brief details of representative undertakings:

Railway	Gauge	Length (miles)	Date of Opening	Cost £ per mile	Remarks
Cambeltown & Machrihanish	2ft 3in	6	1906	4,910	Mainly "easy" agricultural country. Pass. traffic about 75% of whole.
Derwent Valley	4ft 8½in	16	1913	7,566	"Easy" agricultural country. Steepest gradient 1 in 150.
East Kent	4ft 8½in	10	1916	25,262	Rolling country. Traffic mainly coal.
Clogher Valley (Ireland)	3ft 0in	37	1887	3,333	Wide Valley. Considerable part of line laid on public roads.
Cork & Muskerry	3ft 0in	18	1887	4,225	"Easy agricultural country."
Sand Hutton	1ft 6in	7.5 (part)	1922	4,400 (approx.)	Rolling country with stretches of 1 in 80.

The permanent way of the S.H.L.R. consisted of steel flat-bottomed rails weighing 20 lb. per yard, secured by spikes to wooden sleepers measuring approximately 3ft × 7in × 5in (also 3ft × 8in × 4in). These were mostly cut locally, although some were obtained from Escrick, a village on the opposite side of York, and transported in the old open-fronted Daimler lorry used on the Sand Hutton estate. The rail came from Robert Hudson Ltd., Leeds, who supplied about 10 miles of it, and also all the pointwork. All points were hand operated by throw-over levers, and were locked in position when passenger trains were running. The ballast consisted partly of gravel, and partly of ashes and cinders, the latter gave the smoother running, and later the gravel ballast also received a top dressing of ashes. It will be seen that the permanent way was very substantial for so small a railway, and it was, in the earlier years at least, quite satisfactory. Later on, particularly on sections where there was a certain amount of clay, and in the cuttings near Bossall, some trouble was experienced after heavy rain with the sleepers sinking, and the track going out of alignment, and despite rectification of the trouble in drier periods, it was very liable to recur after more rain.

Early days on the 18in gauge, showing Mr. Batty and an unidentified 0-4-0WT. Note the stovepipe chimney without cap or spark arrester. (K.E. Hartley collection)

The S.H.L.R. was a single track throughout, and although run-round loops were of course provided at the termini, and also at Sand Hutton Depot, there was never any question of two trains meeting, or crossing, on the line. Thus, under the conditions of Light Ralway Order, signals were not required on the railway, and they were not in fact provided. When passenger trains were run, however, in addition to the locking of all points on the main line, as a safeguard to working over the common line between White Sike junction and Warthill a somewhat elementary signalling arrangement was in force. The driver of the passenger train carried with him on the engine a red disc, which, when proceeding to Warthill, he hung upon a white painted board erected at the junction. This indicated to a driver arriving later from the Claxton branch that the section ahead was occupied, and he had to wait until the passenger train returned and its driver removed the disc from the board. Instructions to this effect were inscribed on the board. It was the practice to allocate engines to a particular section of the railway, and their working was confined to this section only for that day.

Altogether, a total of six public highways was crossed on the level, and at none of these were gates erected, although cattle grids were provided as necessary, and warning boards were put up, as detailed in the Order, to warn road traffic. On the railway itself the boards appear to have carried the symbol VVV in black on a white ground, and not the definite figure 4 which was the specified speed at, or approaching, level crossings. The maximum running speed allowed on the railway was 12 m.p.h.

Buildings on the line were the bare minimum necessary, and were of a Spartan simplicity. Easily the largest and most important of them was the Depot at Sand Hutton. Measuring 60ft 9in × 21ft overall was a brick-built base 4ft in height, on which was erected the curved steel framework and corrugated sheeting of the superstructure, with ends of timber and a large wooden clerestory running the full length. This clerestory had twelve bays, six of which were glazed, while the alternating portions each had four horizontal louvres for ventilation. At the Warthill end of this shed two tracks entered by independent, 7ft wide double doors, and these provided ample accommodation for the locomotives and passenger coach. Equipment consisted only of hand tools, a bench, and small drills, and the sole provision for lighting was by hurricane lamps and hand torches. A pit was dug outside the

ESMÉ and the coach at Bossall, showing Sir Robert and Lady Esmé Walker beside the coach.
(K.E. Hartley collection)

ESMÉ outside Sand Hutton Depot. Sidings are shown in the background, the main line being behind the photographer.   *(H.G.W. Household)*

shed but got used only occasionally as when there was work to do underneath the locos; in readiness for boiler inspections, for example, the method was to raise the engines either by screw jack, or by levering up with lengths of rail and sleeper packing.

Somewhat surprisingly, the only shedding provided for the goods traffic was on the Claxton branch, where, at the terminus abutting Whinny Lane, there was a small brick-built shed, with corrugated sheet roof, and a platform inside. A single track ran into this shed, and two sidings and a run-round loop completed the layout here. At Warthill, the only building was a small wooden hut which adjoined, and housed the mechanism of the 6 ton rail weighbridge supplied by W. & T. Avery Ltd. of Birmingham. There were, however, two or more small store-places formed in the brickwork of the loading ramp, probably used mainly for tools, etc.

The Company was not obliged to provide any shelter for intending passengers, and at Warthill, the usual amenities supplied by the North Eastern Railway served S.H.L.R. travellers also. At Sand Hutton Central, however, a glazed wooden waiting shed was erected by the line-side, and there was a low gravel platform, a few inches high. Seats and automatic slot machines provided minor luxury at this place. A smaller, open fronted shed of lean-to pattern, was provided at Bossall terminus.

Engineering works generally were on a minor scale, as the railway was laid largely as a surface line, particularly on the Warthill—Sand Hutton and Claxton branch sections, where small embankments were about all that was needed. Beyond Kissthorns, en route to Bossall, there were two fairly deep cuttings in heavy clay soil but otherwise there were no earthworks of much note.

Mention has already been made of the bridge which was to have spanned the River Derwent. There were, additionally, three smaller spans, all constructed in similar fashion, with concrete piers carrying four lengths of old main-line rail embedded level with the top surface. The narrow gauge sleepers were laid directly on top of this elementary structure, and clamped thereto with long through-bolts and plates. Two of these bridges were very small affairs of a single span, and crossed large dykes on the mile stretch up past White Sike. The third was larger, and had a length of 40ft. It crossed a large stream—actually, the tiny River Stank—between the Depot and Sand Hutton Central station, and had three spans, supported on four piers. It was sometimes known as the "Forth Bridge", and its lack of any handrail or catwalk probably seemed almost as awe-inspiring to passengers on the little train!

SAND HUTTON LIGHT RAILWAY

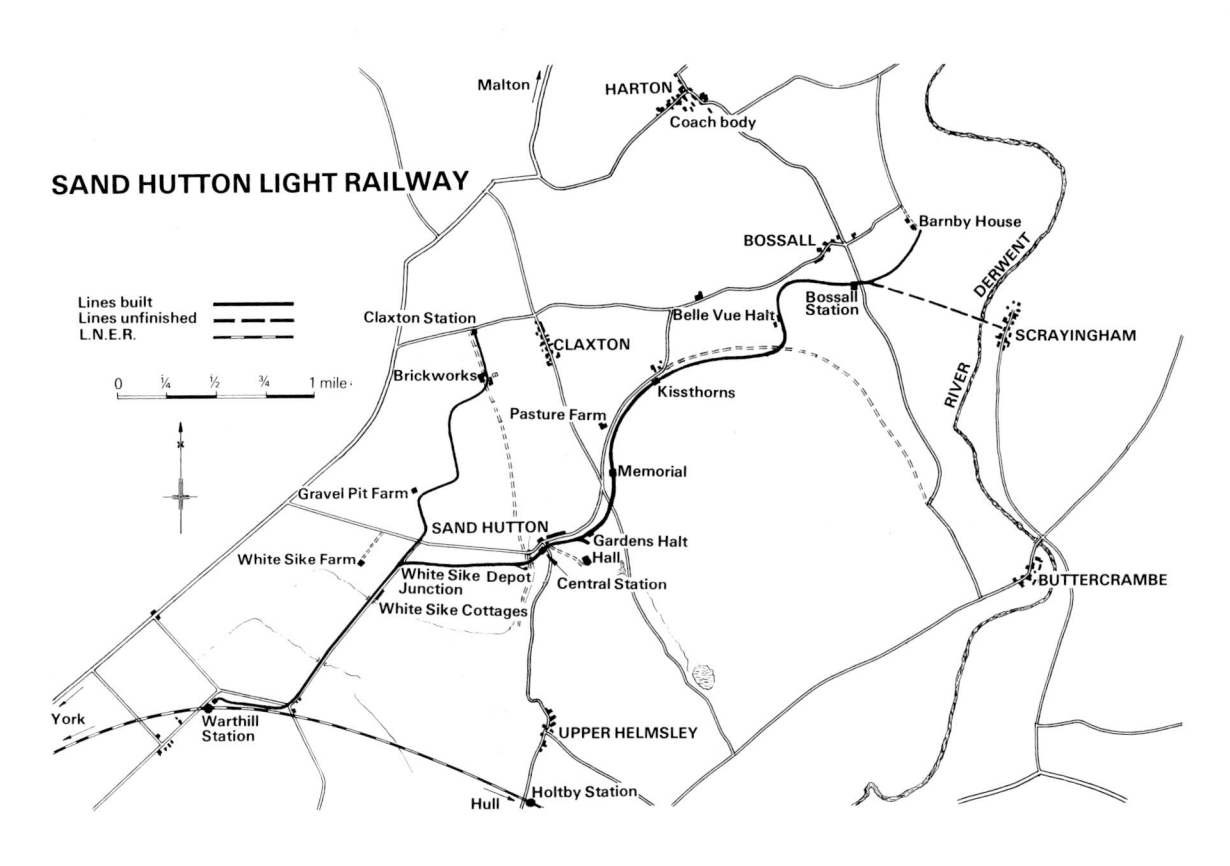

Lines built
Lines unfinished
L.N.E.R.

0 ¼ ½ ¾ 1 mile

Malton — HARTON — Coach body
Barnby House
BOSSALL
Claxton Station — CLAXTON — Belle Vue Halt — Bossall Station — SCRAYINGHAM
Brickworks — Pasture Farm — Kissthorns — RIVER DERWENT
Gravel Pit Farm — Memorial
White Sike Farm — SAND HUTTON — Gardens Halt — Hall — BUTTERCRAMBE
White Sike Depot Junction — Central Station
White Sike Cottages
York — Warthill Station — UPPER HELMSLEY
Hull — Holtby Station

The passenger train, composed as usual of the coach and brake van, standing in the loop at Warthill. July 1927. (H.G.W. Household)

Water supply for the locomotives was as primitive as were other aspects of the railway. One of the main provisions was a specially sunk well at Bossall, into which a bucket had to be dipped, and the contents transferred via a large funnel to the engine. Owing to the limited capacity of the tank (58 gallons) it had to be replenished on every trip. There was a similar open well at Sand Hutton Depot, situated near the run-round loop. An emergency water supply could also be taken at one of the streams near White Sike. It seems strange that less primitive methods were not employed, especially as even on the 15in gauge miniature railway a proper tank had been provided.

There were numerous sharp curves—some of two chains radius—on the railway, for it followed field boundaries to a considerable extent. Gradients west of Sand Hutton were generally very easy; but in the other direction there was a considerable amount of climbing, mostly at 1 in 80, to the summit of the line at Kissthorns, and thereafter, long descents at 1 in 100 and 1 in 80 to Bossall. The most severe climbing, however, was on the Barnby House branch, where the gradient was as much as 1 in 65.

The Light Railway commenced alongside the Station Master's garden at Warthill Station, where a gravel line-side path denoted the S.H.L.R. passenger station. From the dead end, a single set of metals ran some distance before reaching a run-round loop and the goods yard, and continued more or less parallel to the main line for about 650 yards, when it swung sharply to the left on a two-chain radius curve and crossed a public road, not far from Forest Farm, and the main line signal box and level crossing. It was near this point that the single track—on approaching Warthill from Sand Hutton—fanned out into three lines, the line on the left running up a sharp embankment and finishing on a long brick-built loading ramp. The centre line formed a ground level siding, and the remaining track, of course, led to the terminus. Between the high and low level sidings, the N.E.R. provided a standard gauge siding, situated so as to make for easy transference of goods between standard and narrow gauge wagons, and vice versa. After careful consideration, Sir Robert Walker had decided that the best and cheapest method of doing this was by manual labour. Traffic from Sand Hutton went on to the ramp, and was passed down to the standard gauge trucks, whilst inwards traffic was again passed downwards from main line to narrow gauge wagons on the low level siding. Thus, much heavy

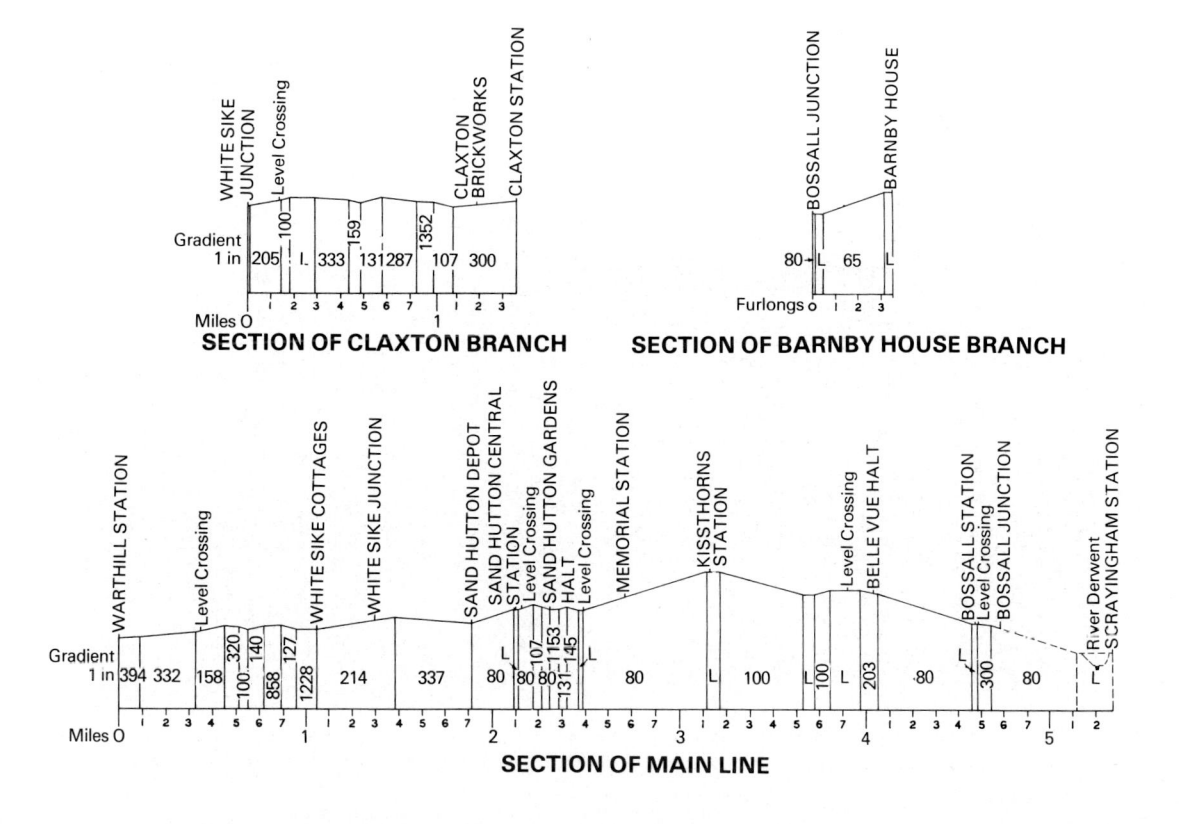

SECTION OF CLAXTON BRANCH

SECTION OF BARNBY HOUSE BRANCH

SECTION OF MAIN LINE

Exchange sidings with the L.N.E.R. at Warthill in 1927. (H.G.W. Household)

The transhipment gantry at Warthill, installed by the L.N.E.R. in July, 1927. (K.E. Hartley)

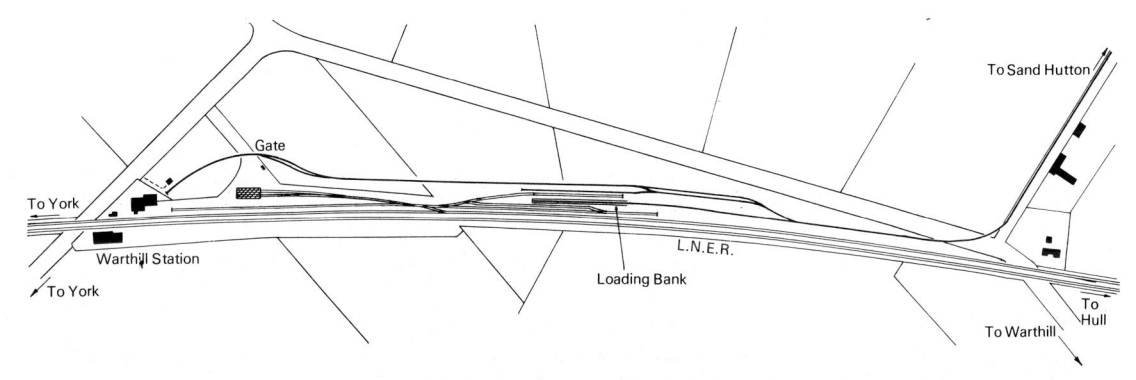

WARTHILL STATION & EXCHANGE SIDINGS

lifting was obviated. The ramp was of such a height that narrow gauge wagon sides let down on to the top of a normal truck side. All traffic was checked at the weigh bridge mentioned earlier. This system remained in use for some years, and all goods were transferred manually, but in 1927, a system of lifting tackle was installed, with the idea of making easier the transhipment of the considerable quantity of bricks from the Claxton Brickworks, and also cutting out the breakages inevitable with the usual "throwing". Erected in July, 1927, by the N.E. Area engineers, the apparatus consisted of a steel framework supported on runners, and capable of being moved along the length of the ramp. It carried tackle to life one ton (tested to 30 cwt) supplied by Alfred Morris, of Loughborough, which could be moved transversely over either standard or narrow gauge wagons. At Claxton, the bricks were loaded on to trays placed in Sand Hutton wagons. On arrival at Warthill the trays were lifted by the tackle, placed over the main line wagon, and the bricks removed and stacked by hand. While fulfilling the objectives above-mentioned, the method was somewhat slow, and regarded by some as a rather mixed blessing.

White Sike Junction, looking north towards Claxton. A Hunslet loco stands on the line from Sand Hutton with the brake van.   (K.E. Hartley collection)

As built

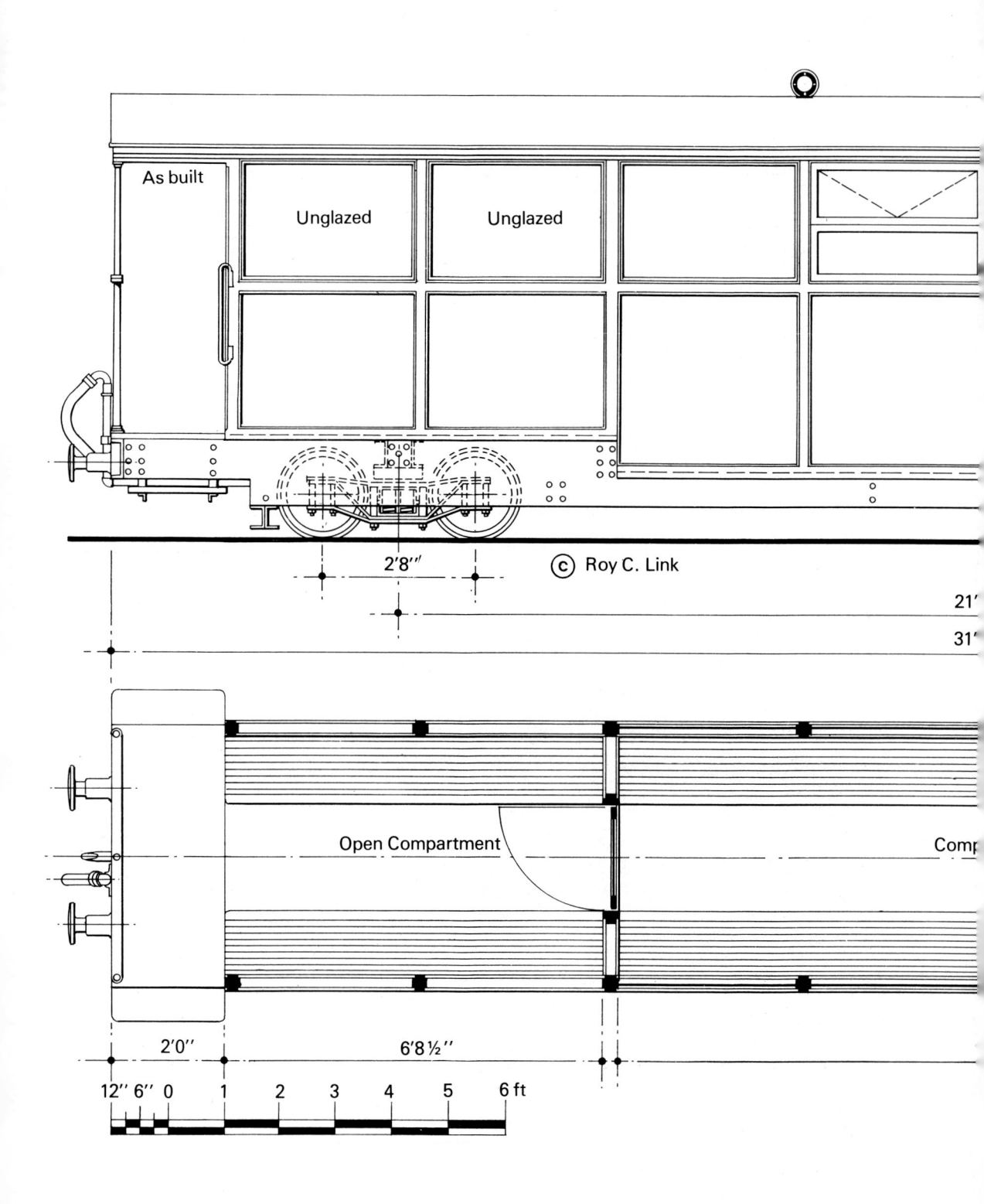

Unglazed

Unglazed

© Roy C. Link

2'8"

21'

31'

Open Compartment

Comp

2'0"   6'8½"

12" 6" 0 1 2 3 4 5 6 ft

As rebuilt

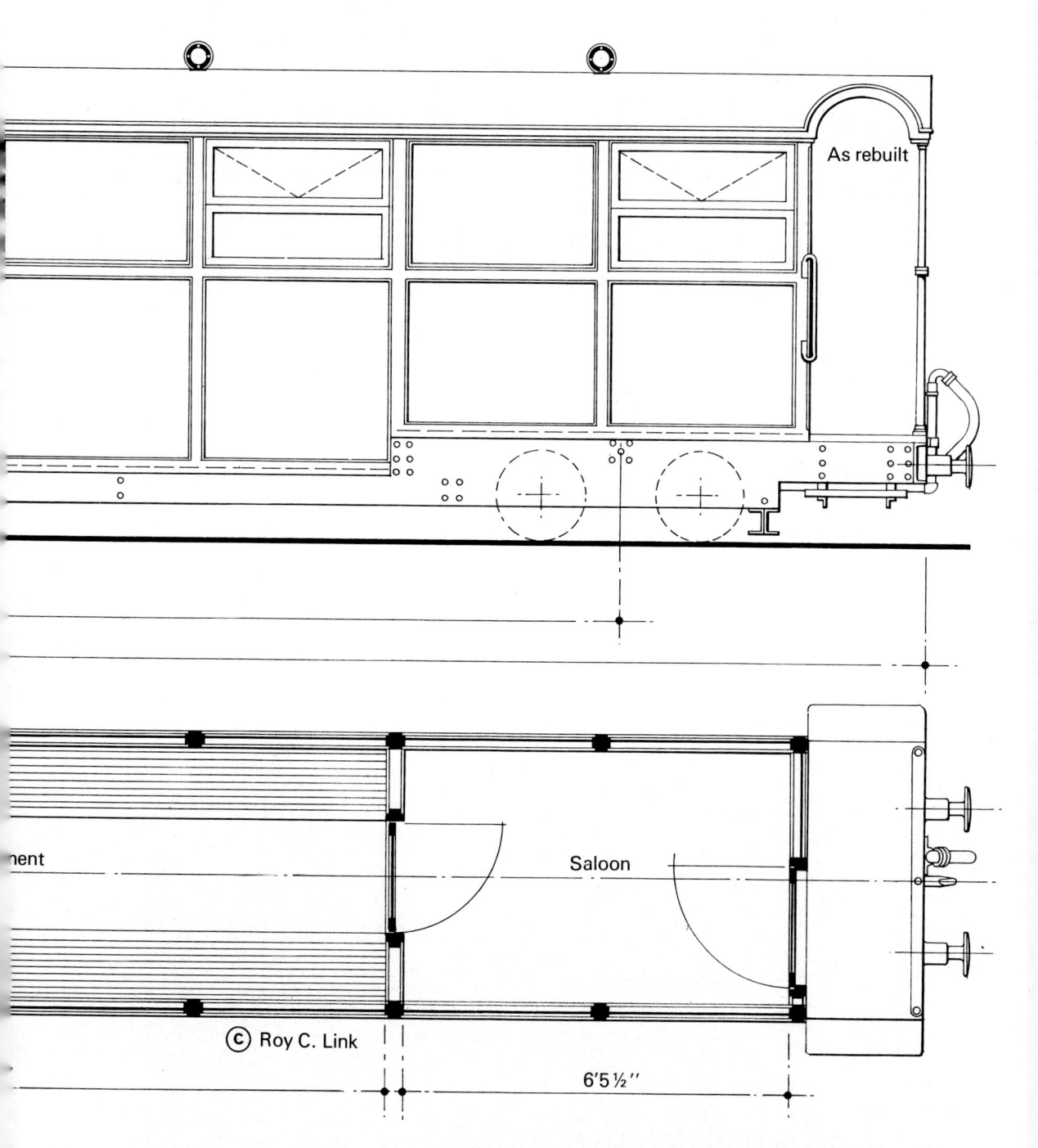

Saloon

© Roy C. Link

6′5½″

S.H.L.R. BOGIE SALOON COACH (from Robert Hudson Ltd drawing and photographs)

A typical scene along the line where the track was laid beside a bridle road through the woods. No. 12, distinguished by the bent front buffer beam, is on the extreme left.
(K.E. Hartley collection)

Claxton station, used for goods traffic only, was the terminus of the branch from White Sike Junction. February 1928. *(H.G.W. Household)*

Sand Hutton Central station, July 1927. (H.G.W. Household)

From the level crossing at Forest Farm, the railway ran alongside a private bridle path for exactly one mile, crossing en route Foss Drain and the little River Stank. The whole of this stretch was practically straight and level. Entering White Sike Plantation, the line passed White Sike Cottages—at which passenger trains stopped if required—and White Sike siding, and at 1 mile 3 furlongs, White Sike junction was reached. Here the Claxton branch continued alongside the bridle road and through the fir woods, and shortly afterwards crossed on the level the public road leading to Sand Hutton village. At 3 furlongs from the junction, Gravel Pit Farm was reached, where a siding was provided, and following a level but sharply curved course along field margins, after a further 5 furlongs came Ox Close siding, and another ¼ mile brought the line into the Claxton Brickworks. Here were a number of sidings serving the various parts of the yard, and after passing by the kilns the line turned sharply to the left, and ran alongside a private bridle road from Sand Hutton to the terminus at Claxton, 1 ½ miles from White Sike Junction.

The main line, after leaving the Claxton branch, turned eastwards into Weed Hill Plantation a delightful area of fir trees and great rhododendron bushes which came up to the line side. On the edge of the forest was the gravel pit, served by a siding, from which much of the ballast used on the Estate and the railway was obtained (after about 1927-28, this traffic went by road) and after leaving the Plantation the track crossed an open piece of ground and came to Sand Hutton Depot. In addition to the accommodation afforded by the Depot building already described, there was a loop line here, and several long sidings. Shortly before reaching the shed the main line commenced to climb a 1 in 80 bank 650 yards in length, and soon after passing the building crossed a bridle road to the Estate kennels and passed over the four-span bridge, curving through woods past the Home Farm and woodyard, to Sand Hutton Central Station. Immediately after this another public road was crossed, the track then cutting across a corner of the park and the carriage drive to the Hall, and following the formation of the old 15in gauge railway for the next ¼ mile. A short branch to the right, on a sharp gradient, served the Hall and gardens. A little distance from the junction was Sand Hutton (Gardens) Halt, and soon afterwards, at 2½ miles from Warthill, a third public road was crossed on the level. Immediately past the crossing, the line curved to the left on a two-chain radius curve, and left the woods.

Now came the start of a long climb of 1,100 yards at 1 in 80 to the summit of the line at Kissthorns. The first portion was on an embankment, skirting the boundaries of fields, and above the public road. At 2¾ miles was Memorial Halt, situated at a fork in the road, wherein stands the Sand Hutton and Claxton War Memorial.

Continuing the climb, Kissthorns was reached at 3¼ miles from Warthill, and 142ft above sea level. This was an important point on the railway and handled heavy traffic from a number of adjacent farms. There was a siding here, but no building of any sort. In passing, it may be mentioned that the line had climbed 74ft above Warthill to reach the summit, from which some fine views are to be had of the Wolds. From Kissthorns, the line descended for almost ½ mile at 1 in 100, crossed a bridle road and traversed a deep cutting shortly before eaching Belle Vue Halt, where a siding was provided to serve a nearby farm. The line thereabouts was more or less level, but after the Halt it recommenced to fall, this time at 1 in 80, right to Bossall, negotiating en route the last of the two-chain curves and a second cutting, and winding along the borders of fields to the terminus. The station, with its waiting shed, was close by the road leading from Bossall village to Buttercrambe, a pleasant little spot, with delightful woods sloping down to the river. Across this road— the last level crossing— was a run-round loop, and soon afterwards the line to Barnby House branched away to the left. The main line continued for a little distance beyond the junction to form a short siding, which indicated the direction of the uncompleted portion which was intended to serve Scrayingham. This unfinished ½ mile was to have crossed the River Derwent at a point 5 miles 1 furlong from Warthill, and terminate a few hundred yards further on in the village. It is understood that the completion of the line was still under consideration shortly before the death of Sir Robert, but that untimely event brought to an end any further thoughts on the project.

The Barnby House branch was 800 yards in length, and climbed steadily all the way from the junction at Bossall, at 1 in 65. The sidings at Barnby House, which was the residence of the late Mr. W. Harrison, a director of the railway, also served other farmers in the area, and in fact the branch was the nearest rail-head for Howsham, a village some 1¾ miles to the north-east. It is interesting to speculate on the amount of traffic which might have originated from the latter source.

The General Manager and Secretary of the Sand Hutton Light Railway was Mr. S.C. Foster, whose headquarters were at the Sand Hutton Estate Office at Claxton (Tel: Stamford Bridge 2) and Mr. Geo. L. Batty was the Engineer. The Company's Solicitors, who also acted for Sir Robert himself, were Messrs. Crust, Todd, Mills & Co., of Beverley. This firm is still in business and kindly undertook a search for old papers relating to the railway during the preparation of this book. But alas, with negative results. By the summer of 1923 there had been several changes in the Company's directors, and not all the parties named in the Light Railway Order remained in office. Mr. W.T. Grundy, one-time General Manager of the Derwent Valley Light Railway, Lady Esmé Walker, and Major P.M. Stuart had now joined Sir Robert Walker and Major H.A. Watson on the Board; but a year later, there was another change, when Major Stuart's place was taken by Mr. W. Harrison of Barnby House. So far as is known, this was the constitution of the Board up to the time of Sir Robert's death.

In the early stages of the railway, and indeed later on, very considerable assistance and advice was given by some of the higher officials of the old North Eastern Railway; and by their subordinates. Indeed, the then General Superintendent of that Company, Major H.A. Watson, C.B.E., was a director from the inception of the light railway. The whole of the survey was carried out by the N.E.R. and aid in one form or another was always readily forthcoming. As Sir Robert stated in his article in *The Railway Magazine* for December, 1924, without his help, the Sand Hutton Light Railway could never have been started, and he had found it impossible to pay adequate tribute to all concerned.

On several occasions, as a gesture of appreciation for the unfailing courtesy and help he had received, Sir Robert invited the Staff at York Station to Sand Hutton, where competitions and games, and a cricket match, followed a trip over the Light Railway, of course, were rounded off by tea on the Hall lawns, and the presentation of prizes by Lady Esmé Walker. Illustrated accounts of two of these occasions appeared in the *N.E.R. Magazine* for December, 1923, and *The Railway Magazine* for October, 1924.

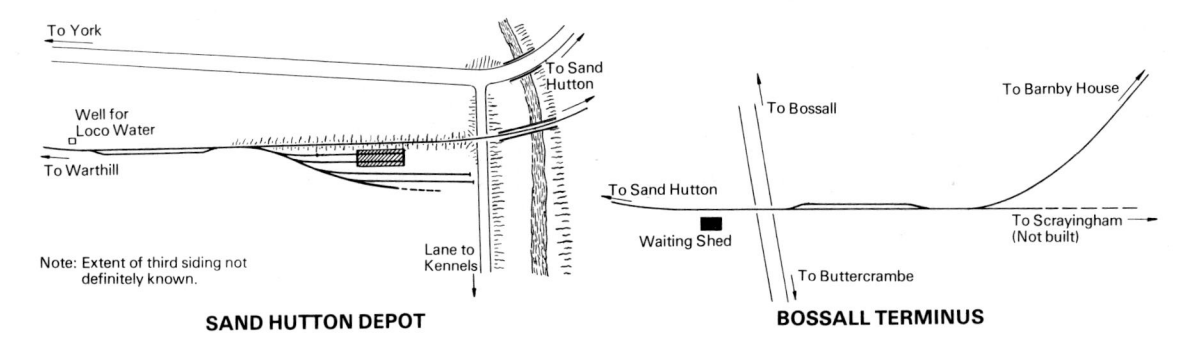

SAND HUTTON DEPOT

BOSSALL TERMINUS

No. 12 among the Rhododendron bushes at Sand Hutton.   *(K.E. Hartley collection)*

ESMÉ and train alongside the waiting shelter at Bossall station.   *(Real Photographs Co Ltd)*

Chapter 7

18IN GAUGE LOCOMOTIVES

ESMÉ at Warthill in July, 1925. The vacuum brake pipe is prominent on the front buffer beam. (K.E. Hartley)

The Deptford Meat Depot, which was to provide the locomotives and rolling stock for the S.H.L.R., was not a product of the First World War as may have been supposed. It was established on the banks of the Thames before the turn of the century, and in 1900 the City of London Corporation built a standard gauge tramway along the public road to connect the Depot with the L.B.& S.C.R. Deptford Wharf branch. Horses were at first used to haul the wagons, but in 1902 The Maudsley Motor Co Ltd of Coventry supplied a petrol-driven locomotive for this work. The 18in gauge system inside the Depot is believed to have been installed while the Corporation was still in charge, but it is not known how this was operated prior to the Government takeover about 1915.

Deptford then became a Special Reserve Depot, operated by the Army, and steam traction was introduced on the 18in gauge railway. The Hunslet Engine Co Ltd, of Leeds, supplied twelve small 0-4-0 well tank engines, the running numbers and works numbers being:

No. 1 works No. 1196 of 1915		No. 5 works No. 1208 of 1916		No. 9 works No. 1288 of 1917	
No. 2	1197 of 1915	No. 6	1209 of 1916	No. 10	1289 of 1917
No. 3	1198 of 1915	No. 7	1210 of 1916	No. 11	1290 of 1917
No. 4	1207 of 1916	No. 8	1211 of 1916	No. 12	1291 of 1917

An illustration of No. 1198 featured in some Hunslet advertisements of the period, and the photograph shows the engine to be smartly painted (in khaki) and lined out, with a polished brass dome cover. The design was generally similar to engines built over a period of years, an early example being JACK (works No. 684 of 1898) now preserved in Leeds.

This loco, and a much later one, GWEN (works No. 1404 of 1920) worked the short 18in gauge line of John Knowles & Co (Wooden Box) Ltd of Woodville, near Burton-on-Trent, until it ceased operation in 1958.

Despite the limitations imposed by such a narrow gauge, the engines had a pleasing, well-balanced appearance, and were possessed of considerable power. The tractive effort, at 75% of the boiler pressure, was 2,192 lb. and the loads which they could handle were stated by the makers to be:-

On the level	115 tons
Up an incline of 1 in 100	55 tons
Up an incline of 1 in 50	30 tons

The frames were placed outside the coupled wheels, and carried a 58 gallon water tank at the front end, under the smoke box. The short wheelbase allowed the engines to traverse with ease a curve of 24ft minimum radius. Apart from the cab, and triangular gusset plates between the tank and front buffer beams, no running plates were fitted, so that the whole of the motion was completely accessible for oiling and maintenance. The buffer beams, unusually for narrow gauge practice, carried large wooden side buffers and hood-and-link couplings. Leaf springs were used for both axles, and cast iron brake shoes acted on all four wheels, operated manually through the usual vertical column and handle. The outside cylinders, 6½in diameter and 8in stroke, were slightly inclined, and the valves were actuated by Walschaerts gear. Lubrication was by Roscoe's No. 1 lubricators, placed one on each side of the very wide smoke box.

The boiler, unlike some narrow gauge designs, was of full locomotive pattern and had an external diameter of 1ft 10¾in (2ft 1¾in over lagging) and carried a working pressure of 160 lb. per sq.in. Twenty-eight 1¾in outside diameter tubes provided 78 sq.ft. of heating surface out of a total of 96 sq.ft. The firebox was of raised, round-topped variety, fairly short but wide, and contributed the remaining 18 sq.ft., while the grate area was 3 sq.ft. One Gresham's No. 3 Combination Injector and an axle driven pump fed the boiler, which carried a centrally-mounted dome, flanked fore and aft by large canister-type sand boxes. Two Ross "Pop" 1½in diameter safety valves were mounted side by side on top of the dome, and the organ-type harmonic whistle just behind them.

The large cab was open at the rear above the low back sheet, which was provided with a sliding panel. A 25-gallon rectangular fuel tank was fitted in the left-hand front corner — the engines were designed for oil firing — and the reversing lever and sanding gear controls were placed in the right-hand side. No steps were provided, as the footplate was but 1ft 9in above rail level.

The weight empty amounted to 5 tons 6 cwts, or 5 tons 19 cwts (6.05t) in working order. The maximum axle load was 3 tons 19 cwts (4.015t), and the lightest rail advisable was 20 lb. per yard. As delivered by The Hunslet Engine Co., the engines had the makers' standard type of chimney with cast iron cap, but at sometime after their arrival at Deptford they were fitted with spark arresters somewhat reminiscent of those used on the older Austrian State Railway locomotives. Whilst doubtless a necessary and worthwhile addition, this fitting could hardly be said to improve the appearance of the engines.

After the end of the War, some of the Deptford equipment became redundant and was in due course put up for sale. As Sir Robert Walker was considering the advisability of using a gauge somewhat bigger than 15in, the Deptford locos and wagons provided an excellent solution, and he lost no time in acquiring three of the engines (Nos. 10, 11 and 12) and a fair amount of rolling stock. This arrived at Sand Hutton early in 1921.

The unsightly spark arresters were very soon removed, and for a short time the engines ran with plain stove-pipe chimneys. This was but a temporary phase, however, for Sir Robert had some beautiful polished copper caps fitted, which completely transformed the appearance of the little Hunslets and, together with the polished brasswork, harmonised well with the deep green livery. The buffer beams were painted black. The outsides of the frames were of the same deep green as the boiler and cab, but between them was finished in signal red.

The price paid for the engines is not known, but it might well be supposed that Sir Robert got a bargain, for they were little worse than new. They gave excellent service, and could handle any Sand Hutton train with ease, although with handbrakes only, braking in bad weather on some parts of the line was a problem. As may be imagined, the combination of a 3ft 6in wheelbase and an overall length of 14ft 1in gave rise to considerable oscillation, and as Sir Robert mentioned, in *The Railway Magazine,* a pair of leading or trailing wheels would have made for much steadier running. The small water capacity of the tank was perhaps more noticeable on the S.H.L.R. than at Deptford, and necessitated a re-fill after each trip. The bucket was generally hung on the smoke-

© Roy C. Link

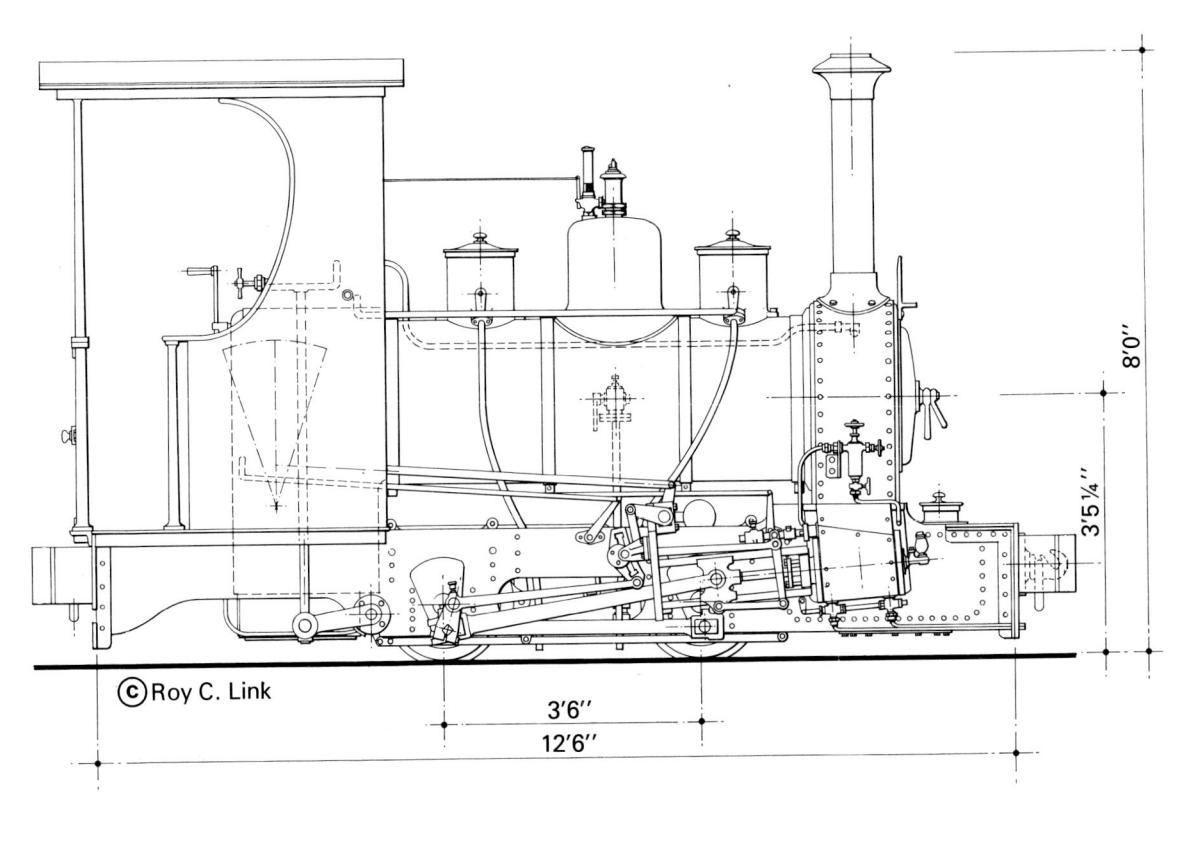

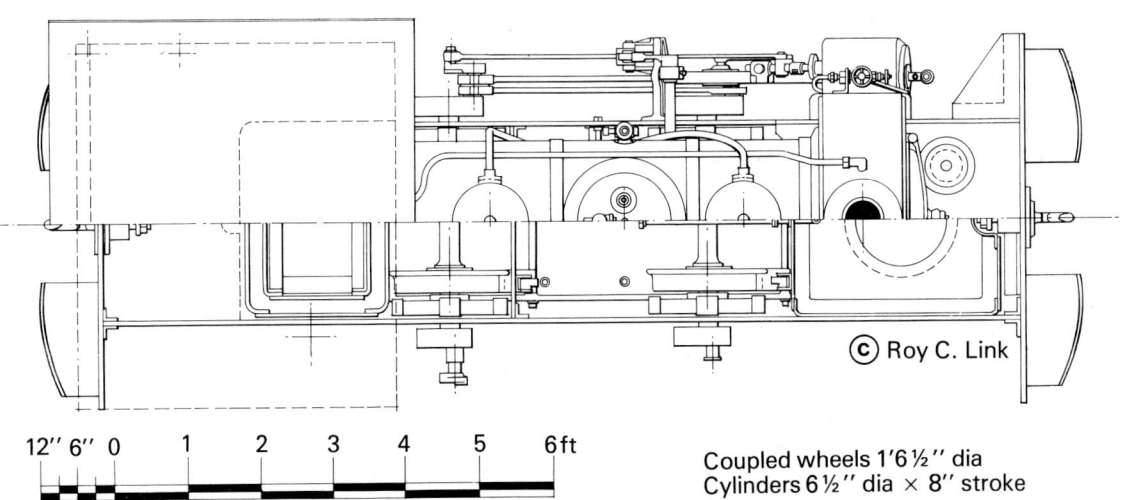

3'6"
12'6"
8'0"
3'5¼"

© Roy C. Link

12" 6" 0 1 2 3 4 5 6 ft

Coupled wheels 1'6½" dia
Cylinders 6½" dia × 8" stroke

**S.H.L.R. 0-4-0 WELL TANK LOCOMOTIVE
(from Hunslet Engine Co Ltd drawing and photographs)**

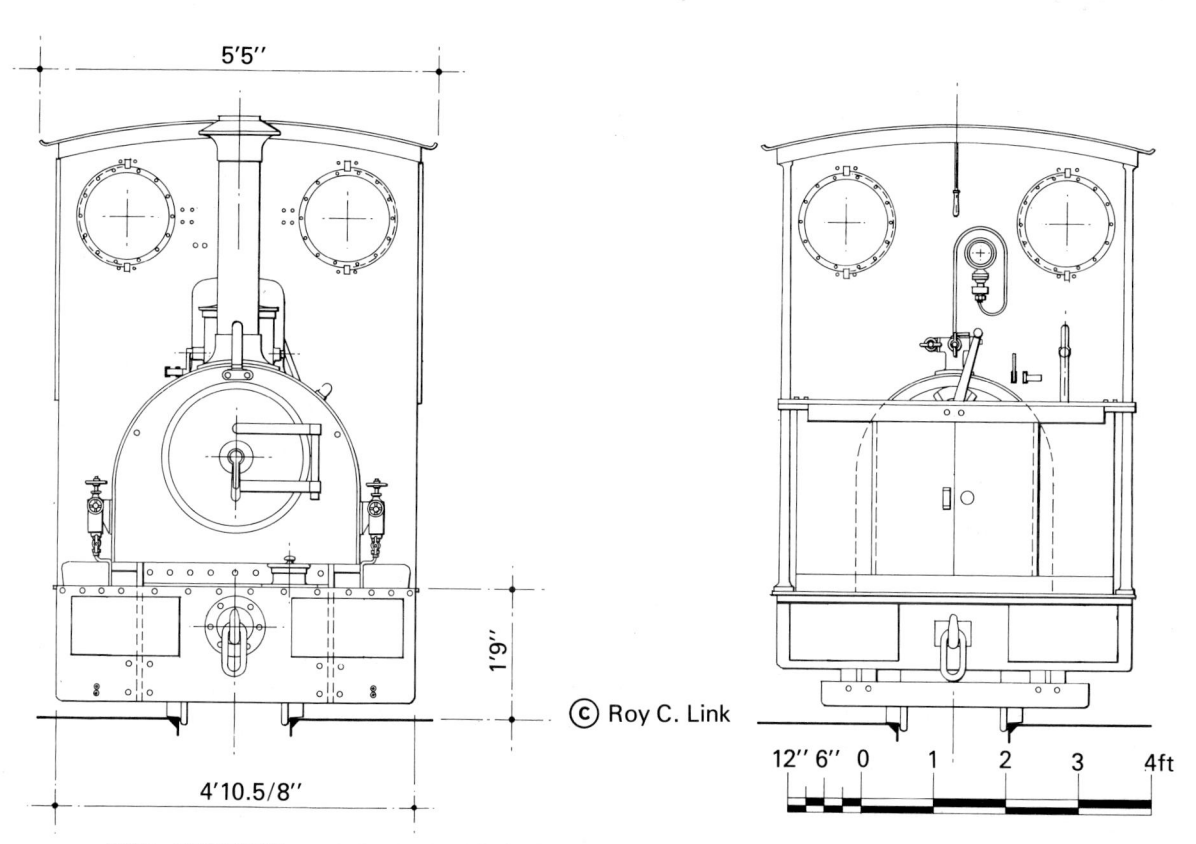

Hunslet 0-4-0WT No. 12 at Bossall station with a train for Warthill. Note the bent front beam, and funnel to allow the tank to be filled by the use of a bucket. (H.G.W. Household)

box door handle, and the funnel left in the filling orifice of the tank. Although originally built for burning oil, the engines were coal-fired at Sand Hutton, and about 4 cwts (0.05t) of fuel was carried in a corner of the cab. Detachable wooden backsheets with round look-out glasses were constructed on the Estate, in order to improve cab comfort when running in reverse. These were secured by four metal clips to the roof stanchions. Another addition, for winter working, was the provision of an acetylene head lamp in front of the chimney — this came from a vintage Daimler open shooting brake, while lamps from an old fire engine served at tail lamp and water gauge light.

Vacuum brake apparatus was fitted to ESMÉ when passenger services commenced, and this was supposed to be the only locomotive used for this work, but in point of fact No. 12 also worked the trains. In view of the light loading, one wonders if the vacuum apparatus was really justified.

In the course of collecting material for this booklet, considerable differences of opinion regarding the locomotive stock were encountered, even among those who had worked on the railway. Sir Robert spoke of three engines in his 1924 article, and The Hunslet Engine Co's records referred to only works Nos. 1289-90-91, although this may have referred to repairs. Again, at the time of Mr. Household's visit, there were but three locomotives. When his article on the railway *(The Locomotive Magazine* October 1928) was in preparation, the typescript was personally vetted by both Sir Robert and his Manager. The number of engines was altered from three to four, and the works No. of the newcomer was inserted (1207 of 1916). This engine was said to have been named ESMÉ and the original trio re-numbered 2, 3 and 4. Although this has usually been accepted as correct, and was quoted in the First Edition, all the Sand Hutton engines retained their Deptford numbers, and were never renumbered by Sir Robert, Thus, it came about that, of his three newest Deptford locos — Nos. 10, 11 and 12 — he named No. 10 (Hunslet 1289 of 1917) after his wife, ESMÉ. The small rectangular nameplates were superimposed on the Deptford Depot plates, hiding the number itself — which explains why no photograph of No. 10 was thought to exist! Photographs of ESMÉ, not available in the early 1960's, clearly show the Hunslet plate carrying 1289 and date 1917. One or two have also since come to light depicting No. 1207 (Deptford No. 4), and do not show any name. The building date of this later addition to S.H.L.R. motive power is given by Hunslet's as 1916 — 1289 (No. 10), 1290 (No. 11), and 1291 (No. 12) all being dated 1917. However, there is no doubt that the final tally of engines was four. No. 1207 was purchased in 1927 and charged to Capital Account. It had been advertised by R.H. Longbotham & Co Ltd in *Contract Journal* and other trade magazines from 1924 and was latterly described as "lying at Deptford". In the *Ministry of Transport Railway Statistics, 1927,* this loco is shown under "Additional Rolling Stock acquired:Locomotives", and the loco stock list shows four engines for the first time. Subsequent statistics all gave the number as four.

Various light repairs to, and re-tubing of, the engines were carried out from time to time, in the 1924-26 period, by The Hunslet Engine Co, who sent fitters to Sand Hutton to do the work. In addition, the following parts were supplied: 15.12.20 — Two pairs of wheels sent by S.H.L.R. to Hunslet for retyring, Works Nos. 1289-1291. Feb. 1921 — Set of Brake Blocks sent to Sand Hutton for Nos. 1289-1291. Aug. 1924 — Vacuum Brake Gear supplied by R. Hudson Ltd, but put on by Hunslet fitter (No. 1289). No major overhaul appears to have been undertaken.

Mr. Batty was, of course, in charge of the engines, and he and Mr. Fred Robinson were the official drivers, but Sir Robert himself would frequently take the regulator, and even in the period shortly before his death, when he was an ailing man, he would forget his troubles when on the footplate. His driving was at times a trifle brisk, with scant regard for doubtful parts of the track — somewhat to the alarm of Mr. Robinson, who slyly nudged the throttle a little towards the closed position! — and caused the immediate question "What's wrong with the damned engine — She's not pulling so well today?"

Following the closure of the railway in 1932, the days of the little Hunslets were numbered. Thos. W. Ward Ltd of Sheffield, who undertook the dismantling of the line, regarded them only as so much scrap metal, and although they were a mere fifteen years old, they came under the torch. To Mr. Robinson, who worked on the dismantling, and who had been instructed in the use of an oxy-acetylene cutter, fell the task of cutting-up the engines — a sad job indeed. The scrap metal was despatched to Sheffield, and so far as is known, not even a solitary maker's plate survived the slaughter.

It is therefore particularly satisfactory, that thanks to the efforts of the Narrow Gauge Railway Society, the older of John Knowles' two similar locomotives should still be in existence, and is now fully restored and on public display in the Leeds Industrial Museum. Enthusiasts will thus be able to recall something of the quaintness of the "Sand Hutton" and its motive power.

Chapter 8: 18IN GAUGE PASSENGER STOCK

The S.H.L.R. possessed only one passenger coach, a large bogie saloon built in 1924 by Robert Hudson Ltd, Gildersome Foundry, Nr. Leeds. This handsome vehicle must certainly have been one of the largest ever built for such a narrow gauge—it would not, indeed, have been out of place on certain 2ft gauge lines. It seated 30 passengers in two separate compartments, and there was additionally a small private saloon, with movable chairs seating a further six persons.

Constructed on the "well" principle, the steel underframe, had the side members formed from 6in × 3in and 8in × 3in channel sections, with buffer beams of the larger section. Two transverse 6in × 3in channel members supported each of the bogie pivots. Just in front of each bogie was a steel fender formed of two lengths of 4in × 3in channel and reaching the full width of the underframe. Short, spring side buffers, with 9in diameter heads, were fitted at 2ft 4in centres, and three-link chain couplings were used. The bogies were of the diamond-frame pattern built up from flat bar and channel section, with two large coil springs at each side, and saucer-shaped pivots. The wheels had a diameter of 1ft 6in on tread and the axle boxes were of cast iron. The body was of timber construction with framework of 3in section, and panelled in ¾in ply, while the roof was of 3/8in ply, canvas covered. The flooring was, unusually, planked diagonally. There were six large ¼in plate glass windows on each side, each alternate one having a hinged top section. Hinged doors, 1ft 10in wide, gave access to the private saloon and the large centre compartment, but the semi-open section, which seated ten, was completely open at the end and had no windows, although waterproof curtains were provided. The main compartment had an inside length of 13ft 4in, allowed 6ft 6in headroom, and seated twenty. All the seats were placed longitudinally down the sides of the coach and were of the lath and space pattern—hygienic, if not specially comfortable! Headroom in the two end sections was 5ft 10in and they were 6ft 5½in and 6ft 8½in long inside—the slight difference being due to the absence of any end on the open compartment. There were platforms protected by neat metal fences, at each end of the body, access from rail level being by a single step at each side. Torpedo ventilators in the roofs of the main and private saloons, electric lighting, and vacuum brake gear were fitted. The weight of this interesting coach was 6 tons 5 cwt (6.35t). It was finished in burnt sienna, with the initials "S.H." in gold and brown letters. The underframe and running gear were painted black and the roof was white.

The original drawing of the coach shows the roof to be of uniform elliptical section, and it was in fact delivered in this state as is very clearly shown in an illustration in Hudson's catalogue of the period. A photograph by

Bogie coach loaded on a N.E.R. wagon at Gildersome for delivery to Warthill.
(K.E. Hartley collection)

The Hudson bogie coach as delivered to the railway, with limited headroom at the balcony entrance, later modified by the addition of elliptical arches to the style shown in other views.
(Photomatic Ltd)

The coach body in use as a cricket pavilion at Harton in 1954. The open end was used to house the roller and mower.
(K.E. Hartley)

Saloon end

© Roy C. Link

Section through open compartment

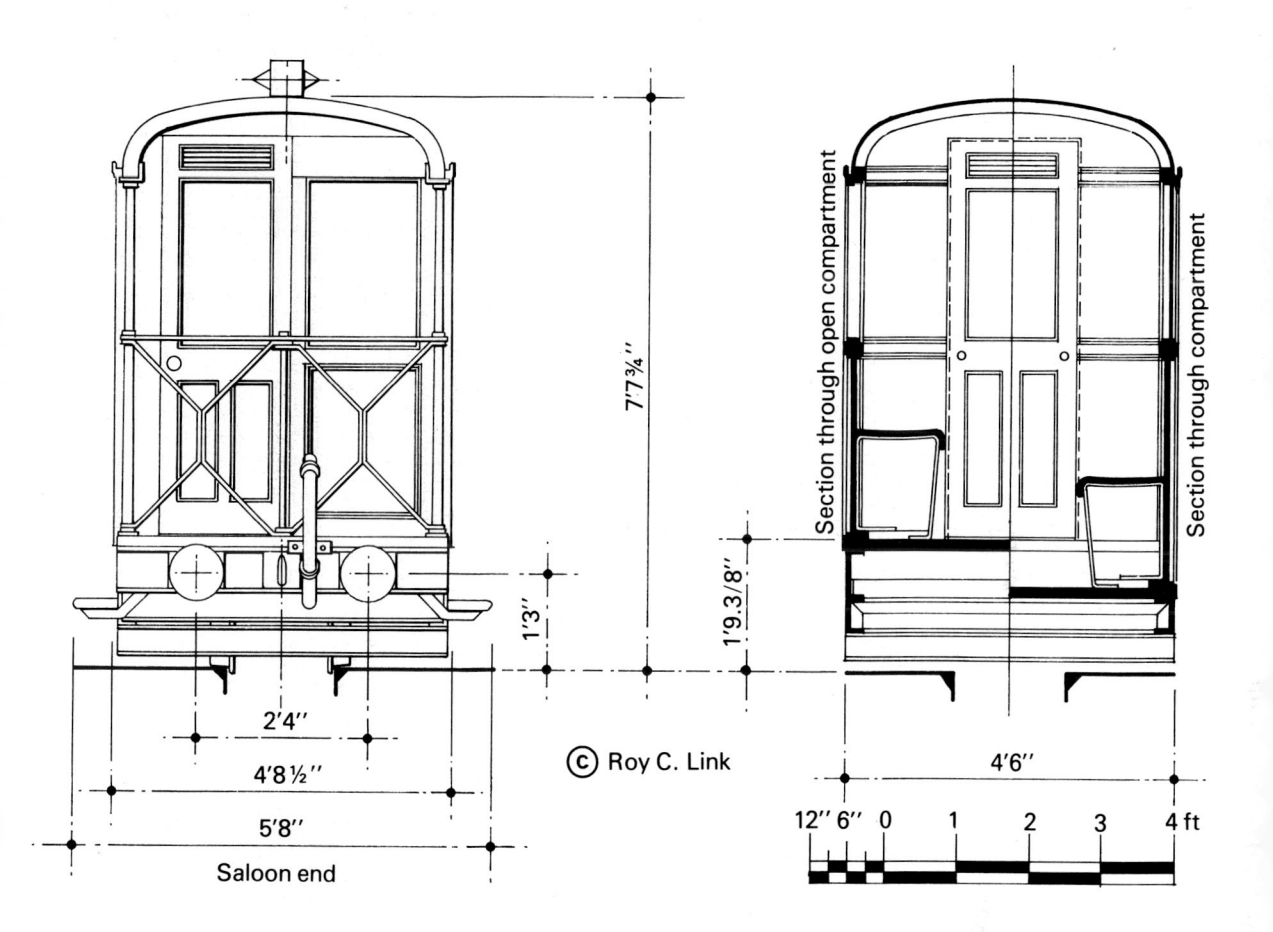

Section through compartment

Mr. H. Speed of York appeared in *The Railway Magazine* for October, 1924. This depicts the York Station staff on the occasion of their second visit to Sand Hutton, in the previous August, standing beside the Light Railway train at Bossall. Again, the continuous elliptical roof is visible. However, it would appear that, before long somebody—possibly even the Board of Trade Inspector—decided that headroom at the entrances to the coach was not as good as it might be, and some little time later the roof was altered. Over each platform a short, transverse section of elliptical roof was built into the original structure giving the coach its long familiar, and totally unique appearance. There is no record of where the work was done, or by whom, but the likely answer is that it was carried out at Sand Hutton. When not in service, the coach was housed in the shed at Sand Hutton Dept.

At one time, the Private Saloon was used as a Buffet, and tea and refreshments were served en route—this novelty was quite popular during the summer months. While the coach doubtless ran smoothly enough, the oscillations and lurchings of the locomotives sometimes caused buffer-locking on curves, and occasionally derailed the leading end of the coach. Experience led to the carrying of a stout length of timber, with which to sort things out again. Under normal conditions this one coach was amply sufficient for the meagre passenger traffic, but its accommodation would be taxed to the limit when fêtes were held, or on special occasions such as the visits of York Station staff, when would-be travellers overflowed into the Brake Van, and even, sometimes into specially prepared wagons.

When the railway closed in 1932, the coach, unlike practically everything else, was not broken up. Or at least, the body was not—presumably the underframe became scrap metal. Mr. Lockwood, a farmer from the neighbouring village of Harton, bought it to use as a pavilion for the Harton Ladies Cricket Club—of which Miss A. Batty was a member—and it was transported to the local cricket field and set on timbers. There, in 1954, the writer found it, looking pretty shabby, in peeling white paint, and with the plywood panelling beginning to disintegrate. The open section, without floor, housed the mower and other equipment, but the other two compartments seemed

The Sand Hutton coach body as fitted to a 60cm gauge underframe for service on the Lincolnshire Coast Light Railway. (W. Woolhouse)

in fair order. It was noted that, despite its age, only one of the plate glass windows was broken. For some reason all the windows on the side remote from the cricket pitch had been blanked off, externally, with corrugated iron sheeting. Internally, the old vehicle still looked to be in good condition, with both seats in the large centre saloon, and the table still in position in the Buffet.

After spending upwards of 35 years in use as a cricket pavilion, the delapidated body was finally transferred to the Lincolnshire Coast Light Railway at Humberston on 17th June 1967 after an enthusiast in the south, who had bought it in 1966, decided that it would cost too much to transport to his home and had donated it to the line for restoration and ultimate use. At Humberston, a new underframe was made from two timber framed former War Department Light Railway D class bogie open wagons. These were stripped to floor level, one bogie on each was removed, and the solebars were reduced in length. New headstocks were then fitted and the half-frames were butt-jointed together. Steel plates were bolted along the sides of the solebars and finally tie bars similar to those on the reconstructed Ashover coaches were fitted. The result was a sound workmanlike job and the body was mounted on the frame when it eventually reached North Sea Lane. In the interests of safety a single floor level was decided upon in preference to the original raised sections at each end, so fillers were jused where the bogies had been. The removal of the metal and old plywood sheeting, a rather formidable job as it turned out, revealed that the framework was in remarkably good condition and it was subsequently re-panelled with new plywood sheets. New iron handrails and fences for the end platforms were made to the original drawing of the coach which, with seating and details replaced, was finished in a rather pleasing light brown shade, with black underframe and running gear and the roof a creamy white. One or two windows had long been broken, so when these were about to be replaced, the opportunity was taken to dispense with the three small hinged upper sections on both sides. The coach is now reasonably close in overall length and height to the Ashover coaches. It was quite some time before I was able to enjoy a ride in this unique carriage, but I did finally manage this on 22nd September 1974 when I sampled all three sections, the private saloon, main saloon and semi-open portion. The running was satisfactorily smooth and steady—much more so I suspect than it had been on the S.H.L.R. shortly before 1930.

Chapter 9

18IN GAUGE GOODS STOCK

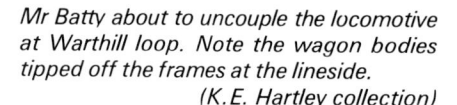

Mr Batty about to uncouple the locomotive at Warthill loop. Note the wagon bodies tipped off the frames at the lineside.
(K.E. Hartley collection)

The wagon stock of the S.H.L.R., like the locomotives, came from Deptford and totalled 75 vehicles. They had been built in May 1915, by P. & W. Maclellan Ltd, of Glasgow, and were of very substantial construction. Basically the design was of a simple four-wheeled underframe, on which a demountable, drop-side body rested on locating bearers. This factor was to prove very convenient on the Sand Hutton line, as it allowed the rapid improvisation of special wagons for exceptional loads.

The underframe was built of timber, the side members being 3½in wide × 4½in deep, and measuring 7ft 0in long over the dumb buffers which were integral with the solebars. They were held apart by massive buffer beam-cum-stretchers, 8¾in × 4½in in section, tenoned-in at each end, and with an additional 3in × 3½in central cross member. A 3/8in × 4½in mild steel plate, 6ft 0in long, was bolted to the outside of each solebar, and a 3/8in × 4in × 1ft 2½in plate armoured the outside faces of the end cross members and carried the three-link drawhooks, the shanks of which passed through the timbers. Coil springs were fitted to absorb the shock on starting. This very solid structure was braced together by a pair of ¾in diameter through bolts, running the length of the wagon inside the wheels, and passing through the buffer beam plates. A single 5/8in through bolt passed transversely through the underframe at its mid-point. Pairs of 5/8in fang-bolts, dogged and bolted to the end timbers, secured these to the side members. Filling-in pieces combined with the ends of the solebars to form the dumb buffers, which were of course sheathed with ½in mild steel plate.

The 1ft 6in diameter disc wheels were arranged on a wheelbase of only 2ft 0in, and the axle journals ran in plain bearings. Uniquely, these latter were not separate items, but were cast in pairs, integral with a massive webbed sub-frame, which was secured to the underside of the solebars by four bolts. No springs were fitted, but the whole construction was so rugged, and the wheelbase so short, that they were not at all necessary.

Two transverse members 4ft 2in long and 4½in deep, mounted on top of the underframe, carried the body. They tapered from 4½in at the bottom to 3½in at the top and carried a locating block centrally secured to their outside faces. The body itself was built of 2in timber, with three-plank sides 2ft 6in deep. The sides were in one section, and were hinged at their bottom edges, being held in a horizontal position by chains, when necessary, for loading or unloading purposes. Two U shaped steel bars, ¾in thick by 4in wide, centred 2ft 6in apart, passed beneath the body and up each end to terminate in lifting eyes above the woodwork. It would appear that at Deptford bodies were removed from the underframe by crane, complete with load, but this was not done at Sand Hutton.

47

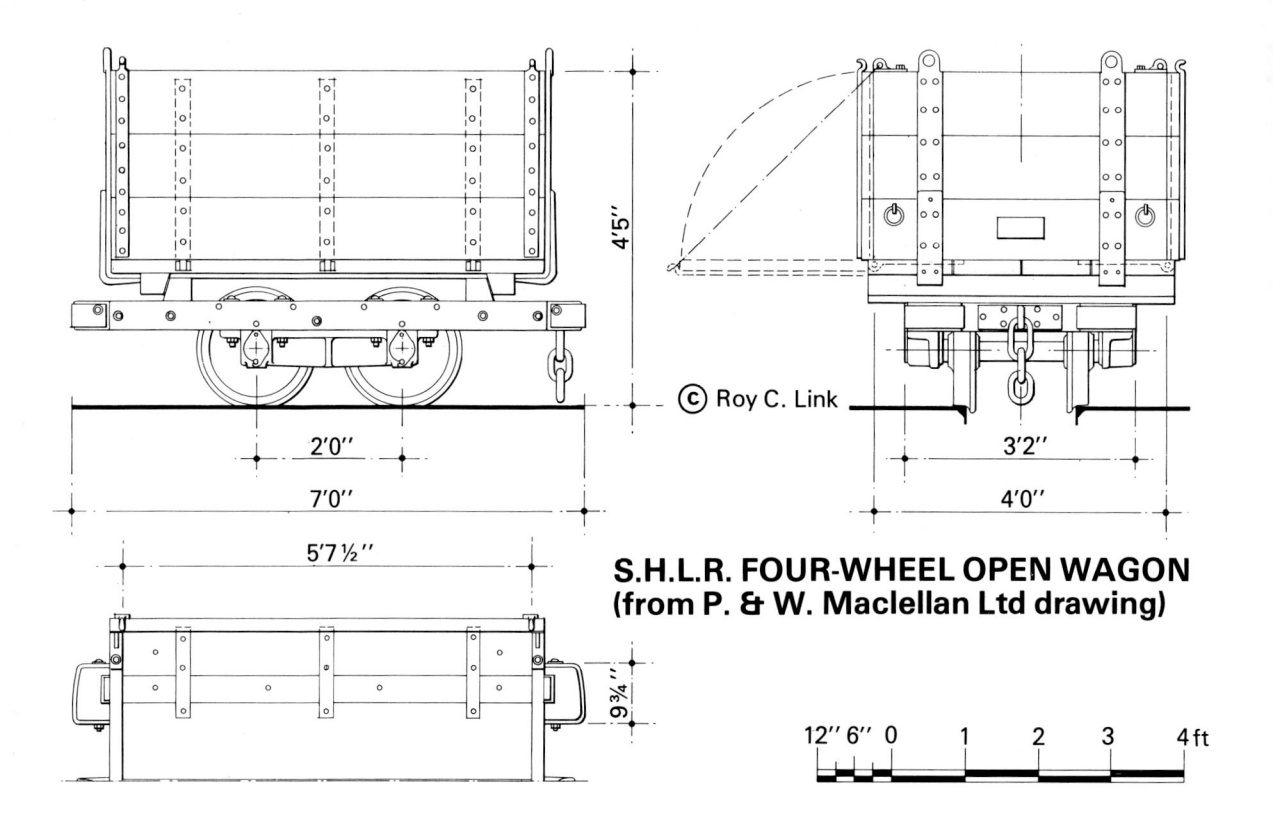

**S.H.L.R. FOUR-WHEEL OPEN WAGON
(from P. & W. Maclellan Ltd drawing)**

© Roy C. Link

Four-wheeled open wagon 18 at Warthill in July 1925. (K.E. Hartley)

No. 11 outside Sand Hutton Depot with a train of wagons loaded with sacks of farm produce.
(K.E. Hartley collection)

The rated load for these wagons was 2½ tons, and the tare averaged 1 ton 4 cwt—an indication of their solid construction. No brake of any kind was fitted. They were painted grey, and bore numbers in white, but no lettering denoted their ownership. On the S.H.L.R. the following were typical loads for a wagon—750 bricks (about 2 tons 5 cwt—2 tons 9 cwt); 40 bags of potatoes; 1 ton of Sugar Beet. For exceptional loads such as timber and hay the underframes of two of these wagons would be used, coupled by a long bar giving a total length of about 18ft. Special bodies—or racks, as they were called locally—were constructed, as required, at the Estate Wood Yard for the hay and clover traffic. These measured 16ft long, by 6ft wide, and could carry 70 trusses of hay. One of these bogie wagons could carry about 3 tons 10 cwt of clover—a standard gauge wagon load.

After the closure, all these wagons were broken up at Sand Hutton, the woodwork being burnt, and the scrap metal sent to Ward's works.

There was one other vehicle on the railway, a neat brake-cum-parcels van, built specially by Robert Hudson Ltd, in June 1923. This van had a steel underframe, and a screw handbrake which acted on all four wheels. The body, which was of timber, had a sliding door on each side, and an end door opening on to the single open platform. Dumb buffers and chain couplings were employed, but vacuum brake gear was not fitted. The pay load was 4 tons, and the tare weight about 1 ton 16 cwt. The height was slightly less than that of the saloon coach, but unfortunately, the drawings of this vehicle no longer exist, and dimensions are not available. The finish was grey, with white lettering and black underframe and running gear. This van seems to have been used on all the passenger trains, for the conveyance of perishable goods, etc., but was not always attached to the goods trains—at least, not the lighter ones. With its very narrow gauge, and considerable overhang at the ends, the riding qualities of this vehicle must have been a trifle lively on the rougher sections of the line. After the dismantling of the railway, the body was acquired by a Sand Hutton resident and used as a hen house. This man left the district some years ago and the final fate of the van is unknown, but it seems likely that it ended up as firewood.

A rather surprising item appears in the *M.O.T. Railway Statistics 1927,* for the brake van appears under both the Passenger and Goods Stock Returns. It is extremely unlikely that two vans were on the line during this one year only and there is no evidence of any sort available to support the M.O.T. statistics on this point.

Brake and parcels van, presumably at the Gildersome works of Robert Hudson Ltd before delivery.
(K.E. Hartley collection)

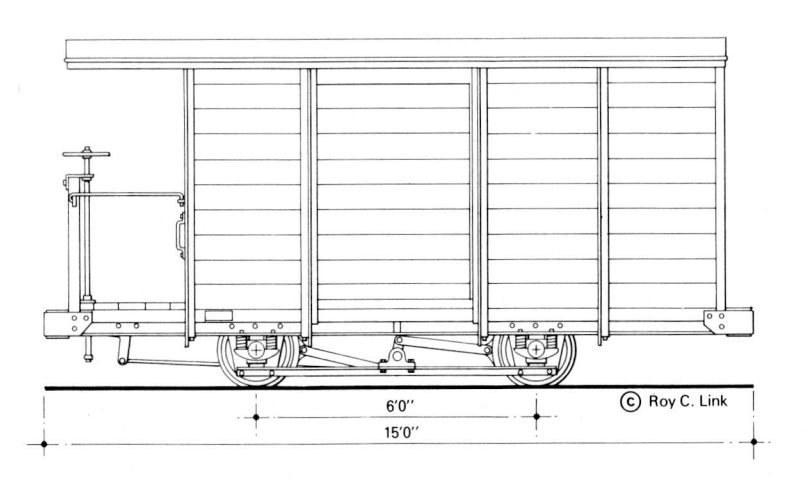

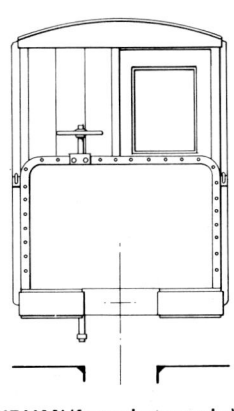

6'0"
15'0"
© Roy C. Link

S.H.L.R. BRAKE VAN (from photographs)

Chapter 10
TRAFFIC AND OPERATION

The primary object of the railway was to provide a cheap means of transport for the produce of the farms it served, and in the other direction, the carriage of coal, fertilisers, etc., and general goods. In addition, of course, it handled the entire output of the brickworks at Claxton. In the early post-war years, country roads generally were in very poor shape, and quite unfitted to the heavy and cumbersome motor lorries of the time, whilst country bus services were virtually non-existant. Thus there seemed to be a reasonably good future for the railway, and in fact the first few years saw the line carrying a considerable traffic, with two engines in steam daily.

"**CIRCULAR LETTER issued from the North Eastern Rly. H.Q. Offices, York** announcing the opening on 3 April 1922 of the Sand Hutton Light Rly for Goods Traffic, etc. including Minerals & Parcels.

Transhipment is required at Warthill, and goods requiring use of crane unsuitable.
Enquiries to be made before consigning bulky articles over 18" gauge Rly.
Through rates will not be quoted for any description of traffic.

Parcels & Miscellaneous Traffic to be way billed and dealt with as "Warthill, N.E.R."

Ordinary Live Stock NOT received as forwarded, but small animals packed (e.g. pigs in crates) may be sent.

GOODS & MINERAL: All traffic for Light Rly to be ticketed to "WARTHILL, N.E.R." for the point on the Light Rly concerned (e.g. "Warthill for Bossall"), and invoiced to "Warthill, N.E.R.", by authorised routes, at rates noted with that Station.
TRAFFIC for CLAXTON, BOSSALL, and SAND HUTTON, not specifically consigned to a North Eastern Station, should be forwarded to the Light Rly Co's station "via WARTHILL, N.E.R."

ALEX WILSON	A.E. WILLIAMS	KENELM KERR
Chief Goods Manager	Accountant	Passenger Manager

ESMÉ at the head of the passenger train leaving Warthill station loop.
(Real Photographs Co Ltd)

The main outwards agricultural traffic consisted of potatoes and general produce from the various farms—most of them had a siding laid in—whilst a considerable amount of hay and clover came from the Barnby House branch. Additionally, after about 1927, sugar beet from a specially-installed siding near White Sike brought in useful revenue, about 300 tons being carried in one season. Six narrow gauge wagons of beet comprised the usual load for a standard gauge truck. In the return direction, flour, feeding stuffs and artificial manures, as well as coal and general merchandise, provided the traffic.

On the Claxton branch, at the height of activity, a matter of 20,000 bricks per day were transported to be either handed over to the L.N.E.R. at Warthill, or taken to Claxton terminus for distribution by road lorries—rather surprisingly there seems to have been no proper road to the brickworks, although they were comparatively near to Whinny Lane. As may be expected, coal provided a fair proportion of the inwards traffic on the branch, and 50 tons per week were taken to the brickworks alone.* Coal provided the best class of traffic in the early days, and in the first twelve months of operation, ending April 1923, 1,318 tons were carried—this before completion of the railway. Agricultural traffic was at first disappointing, due in part to its seasonal nature. On the whole local farmers supported the railway fairly well, and there were some to whom its eventual closing was a sad blow. Round about 1927-8, with improvements to both roads and motor vehicles, other farmers adopted road transport and gradually this traffic began to fall away from the railway. Bricks continued to be handled in large quantities for some time, however, until somewhat abruptly production at the yard ceased owing to lack of suitable basic material. A considerable sum of money had been spent on installing modern Belgian machinery not very long before, and it is rather surprising that a possible shortage of clay seems to have been overlooked. The loss of this substantial traffic was a serious blow to the railway, which was already facing increasing road competition, as well as the inevitable results of acute agricultural depression. With the death of Sir Robert, early in 1930, the mainspring of the railway was gone, and although the various events just detailed did not cause the immediate closure of the railway, by early 1932 it was obviously impossible to carry on much longer.

*Claxton Brickworks was another venture in which Sir Robert Walker was interested. It was taken over about 1927 by the Stairfoot Brickworks Co., and was managed for some time prior to its closure by the late Mr. Henry Oakland, who subsequently set up the works of Henry Oakland & Sons Ltd at Escrick, on the main York to Selby road. This firm is now carried on by his son, Mr. H.E. Oakland, and considerable modernisation of the plant has been effected. The works were connected to the clay pit by a 2ft gauge railway about 500 yards long, worked by two Motor Rail "Simplex" locos, but this closed in June 1979.

A coal train at Claxton Brickworks, November 1927. (H.G.W. Household)

A train at Sand Hutton Depot made up of two open wagons and two hay racks on wagon frames. *(K.E. Hartley collection)*

The method of working the traffic, as between the Light Railway Co. and the farmer, was very fully dealt with by Sir Robert Walker in *The Railway Magazine* for May 1924, and appears to have satisfactorily stood the test of time. It may be explained thus:-

When a farmer sold his crop to a dealer he told the latter that he wished to send his goods via the Light Railway, and that forwarding instructions should be sent to that Company's office. As soon as definite forwarding instructions were received the Light Railway advised the farmer, and asked him to specify the exact date when he wished his produce to be despatched. The Light Railway then arranged for a standard gauge wagon, sheets, and if necessary sacks, to be at the junction, and supplied narrow gauge wagons to the farmer's siding. On the specified day the farmer loaded his produce into these, and filled in the consignment note which he handed over to the Light Railway representative. The goods were then taken over the Light Railway to the junction, transhipped and sheeted, if required, and the consignment note handed over to the junction stationmaster. The main line railway took over and ticketed the wagon, which was then ready for the evening pick-up goods. The Light Railway foreman loader entered the wagon number and any special remarks on the consignment note and returned it to the Light Railway office. The latter advised the farmer that his goods had been sent off according to his instructions, and gave details of the consignment and the wagon number. These arrangements had already been in use as between the Derwent Valley Light Railway and the N.E.R., and Mr. S.R. Wade, late of British Railways was transferred from Cliff Common to Warthill for the opening of the S.H.L.R., to deal with the accountancy arising from the new line. Goods trains were not run to any particular timetable, but as traffic demanded. Through goods trains were worked at passenger train schedules, with a 12 m.p.h. maximum speed.

Turning now to the passenger traffic, this never was, by the very nature of things, able to attain to any great proportions. Colonel J.W. Pringle, C.B., R.E., the Chief Inspector of Railways for the Ministry of Transport, inspected and passed the line for Passenger Traffic, and this commenced on October 4th, 1924. The service was according to the published timetables, a Saturdays only one, although it is understood that at one time there was also a service on Wednesdays. The buffet car was in use on both services for a period. Local passengers were not numerous — hardly surprising, as the area served had no large villages — but one regular traveller was the Vicar of Bossall, a bearded gentleman who remained faithful to the railway to the end. It would seem that the bulk of the passengers carried were those attracted by the unusual character of the line. Although the regular public service was not an outstanding success, on Bank Holidays, fête days and special occasions such as organised visits by parties, Sir Robert would run trips from Sand Hutton down to White Sike, and up to Kissthorns, for a fare of 6d (2½p) and the coach and van were frequently packed with passengers enjoying the novel experience. The proceeds on these occasions were devoted to charities, notably the Coldstream Guards Welfare Association. Tickets were issued on the train by a Conductor-Guard, and were of thin card rather like tram tickets. Although a complete list of fares is not available samples are quoted herewith: Warthill to Memorial (blue) single 4d (1½p); Warthill to Bossall (buff) 8d (3p). These are 1927 prices, but probably the fares never varied during the railway's existence. As a point of interest, "Warthill to Bossall" tickets Nos. 944/5 were issued on July 23/27, and a similar ticket, No. 1000, was not issued until November 26th of the same year. One may compare the above charges with those set out in the Order.

The journey time from Warthill to Bossall was officially 40 mins., but in actual practice much quicker running was often made. The timings were so arranged as to give good connections with N.E.R. trains to and from York. It will be recalled (Chapter 6) that the S.H.L.R. passenger station at Warthill had but a single track. Trains from Bossall and Sand Hutton therefore halted at the passing loop some distance away, where the loco. ran round its train, and then propelled it into the terminus. A practice not uncommon with the local people, when the passenger service was not running, was to use the goods train, or a light engine, a roughish footplate ride being preferable to a long trudge along the country roads, and sometimes this unofficial taxi service was put to unusual use. On one occasion, for example, Mr. Robinson was sent with an engine to take the local nurse to an urgent maternity case some distance down the line. Despite his best efforts, however, they were greeted on arrival at the house by a voice saying, "Too late! Baby's here!" — but almost simultaneously came another voice "No, you're not, there's another one due!"

It has been said that "the line wasn't really fit for goods traffic, let alone passengers!" — a reference to its later days, no doubt — but nevertheless, there is no record of anybody ever getting injured. There were, of course, derailments, but never anything of a serious nature. In the early years of her service, No. 12 encountered a tree stump near the lineside and suffered a bent front buffer beam as is evident in various photographs. On another occasion, an engine hauling a couple of 2 ton trucks and a loaded bogie hay wagon came off on a sharp curve in the woods. The track at this point was on a low embankment, and the loco would have toppled over but for her cab, which fortunately came to rest against a tree. The driver decided to hurriedly quit the footplate, from the opposite side, just in case! There is no doubt that towards the end of operations the condition of the track deteriorated, and made the running very unsteady. This was especially so at the Bossall end, and on many occasions the loco seemed in imminent danger of rolling over against the side of the cutting, causing the driver some alarm! But somehow, this never actually happened. More frightening to the footplate crew, however, was a said deficiency in brake power. Handbrakes only on the engines (excepting ESMÉ) did not always give sufficient control over heavy loads down from Kisshorns and Memorial, even when the brake van was attached at the rear. Especially was this so in bad weather, when greasy rails aggravated the trouble. On numerous occasions there was no possibility of stopping at some of the level crossings, and the drill was to hold tight, keep the whistle on full song, and hope that any road traffic would stop before reaching the railway! Luckily, in those days road vehicles were neither fast nor numerous, particularly in this quiet area of Yorkshire, and no collisions actually occurred. But there were anxious moments!

An incident which might easily have had serious results took place one day when Mr. Robinson was down the line with a loco and two wagons, picking up sundry rubbish. He was accompanied by his sister and a young schoolboy from York, who frequently visited the line and rode on the footplate. While Mr. Robinson was busy, some little distance from the engine, he was horrified to hear it start slowly away: the boy, although he had never shown any desire to drive, had opened the regulator, and momentarily panicked when the loco moved off. Too far away to run after and catch the runaway, all that Mr. Robinson could do was to make signs to the lad to close

A heavily loaded special passenger train with ESMÉ at Kissthorns siding one "Fête Day".
(K.E. Hartley collection)

This delightful view, full of atmosphere, shows a passenger train in the woods near Sand Hutton. *(Locomotive Publishing Co, courtesy Ian Allan Ltd)*

the regulator. Very fortunately the youngster understood, and brought the engine to a standstill. But his trip on the railway was over for that day—he was ordered to go home, in dire disgrace, by a relieved, but very shaken driver. Nor was his father gratified by his escapade, and for some time, Sand Hutton was out! Later, the boy was again allowed on the line, but never attempted a second essay at driving.

The timetable for 1924 is as under:-

		A.M.	P.M.	P.M.			P.M.	P.M.	P.M.
Bossall	dep.	8.05	12.20	4.30	Warthill (S.H.)	dep.	1.05	3.05	5.18
Kissthorns	dep.	8.20	12.35	4.45	S. Hutton (Cent)	dep.	1.20	3.20	5.30
Memorial	dep.	8.25	12.40	4.50	Memorial	dep.	1.25	3.25	5.35
S. Hutton (Cent)	dep.	8.30	12.45	4.55	Kissthorns	dep.	1.30	3.30	5.40
Warthill (S.H.)	arr.	8.45	1.00	5.10	Bossall	arr.	1.45	3.45	5.55

Tea and refreshments were provided on the 12.20 p.m., 1.5 p.m., 3.5 p.m., 4.30 p.m. and 5.18 p.m. trains. *Bradshaw* for July 1925, showed similar timings, but with the additional information that the 8.05 a.m. and 3.05 p.m. trains also ran on Wednesdays, and that there were Halts at White Sike Cottages, White Sike Junction, Sand Hutton (Depot), Sand Hutton (Gardens) and Belle Vue.

The L.N.E.R. timetable for July 11th to September 25th, 1927, contains some alterations to the train times, as follows:-

		Weekdays					*Weekdays*		
		P.M.	P.M.	P.M.			A.M.	P.M.	P.M.
York	dep.	12.25	2.47	5.08	Bossall	dep.	9.55	12.20	4.30
Warthill	arr.	12.38	3.00	5.21	Kissthorns	dep.	10.10	12.35	4.45
Warthill (SH)	dep.	1.05	3.15	5.25	Memorial	dep.	10.15	12.40	4.50
S. Hutton (Cent)	dep.	1.20	3.30	5.40	S. Hutton (Cent)	dep.	10.20	12.45	4.55
Memorial	dep.	1.25	3.35	5.45	Warthill (SH)	arr.	10.35	1.00	5.10
Kissthorns	dep.	1.30	3.40	5.50	Warthill	dep.	10.43	1.10	5.22
Bossall	arr.	1.45	3.55	6.05	York	arr.	10.55	1.23	5.34

The Sand Hutton services were shown as Saturdays only. The L.N.E.R. timetable from September 26th, 1927, and *Bradshaw* for both July and November of that year, all do not show any train at 9.55 a.m. from Bossall. Strangely enough, a timetable at Sand Hutton Central station, printed and corrected in ink, marked as commencing October 4th, 1927, showed the 9.55 a.m. ex-Bossall as running, and also the mid-afternoon train as leaving Warthill at 3.05 p.m. once again, and arriving at Bossall at 3.45 p.m. The July *Bradshaw*, incidentally, showed the trains as Weekdays only instead of Saturdays only.

Chapter 11
THE END OF THE LINE

As mentioned in the previous chapter, with the death of Sir Robert, the real driving force behind the line was gone, and a study of the traffic returns for 1930 and the following year shows only too clearly how the affairs of the railway slumped. Although the receipts for 1929 amounted to only £11, as compared with £180 for the previous year, in 1930 there was a deficit of £199. Freight income was over £300 down, and passenger receipts fell from £15 to a mere £1. The actual tonnage carried was little more than half of that in 1929, while passengers had dwindled to 65, as compared with 791. Matters were further in the red by 1931, and despite a much reduced expenditure on working the line there was another deficit of almost £200. Freight carriage amounted to only a quarter of the 1930 tonnage, but surprisingly, the 61 passengers carried appear to have brought in twice the 1930 revenue! The early 1930's were bad years not only around Sand Hutton, but throughout the whole country with unemployment rampant and trade in the doldrums, so that the prospects of the S.H.L.R. ever regaining any traffic appeared extremely remote. Far more likely was it to incur even heavier losses, and the shareholders decided early in 1932 that the only thing to do was to close the railway before more money was lost. Accordingly, a meeting was held at Sand Hutton on March 22nd, 1932, at which it was decided to apply to the Minister of Transport (Light Railway Dept.) for an order authorising the discontinuation of the Railway.*(The Railway Magazine* May 1932.)

The *Yorkshire Gazette* for March 25th, reported on it thus:-

"It is possible that the Sand Hutton Railway, the smallest light railway in this country, running between Bossall and Warthill stations and connecting up at the latter point with the York and Hull branch of the L.N.E.R. will be abandoned.

Sir Robert Walker on the balcony of the brake van, and a member of the Hall staff on 0-4-0WT ESMÉ.
(K.E. Hartley collection)

"At an extra-ordinary general meeting of the Company, held at the Estate Offices at Claxton, near York, on Tuesday, a resolution was passed on these terms:-

"That it is desirable the Company should be wound-up, and that application to the Minister of Transport, under Section 7 of the Light Railway Act 1912, be made accordingly.

"Originally, this little railway linked-up the old N.E.R. and the Sand Hutton estate, with direct access to the Hall and the farm. The idea arose out of a miniature railway which Sir Robert Walker, who died a year or two ago, built round the Sand Hutton Park. This became very popular at fêtes and such-like events, and after the War, Sir Robert Walker deemed the idea worth practical application in other parts of the estate. Consequently, a small company was formed and the railway was built with a total length of seven miles.

"The line was of 18" gauge, instead of the 15" (like that of the well-known Ravenglass and Eskdale Railway) originally contemplated, this being fixed upon in order to take advantage of an opportunity to buy small tank 0-4-0 locomotives and about 75 small box wagons, which during the war had been in Government service for meat carrying purposes.

"The line had conveyed passengers on Saturdays and other special days, but its main traffic was an outward flow of produce (mainly potatoes) with coal and farm supplies coming inward. The stock had been found effective for the purpose to which it had been put. The line had sidings at twelve farms and gardens."

The authority was granted in June, 1932, and all traffic ceased in the same month. In Vol. 22 of the *L.N.E.R. Magazine,* Mr. H.A. Watson (one of the S.H.L.R. Directors) quotes the official date of closure as June 30th, 1932. The M.O.T. Statistics give returns for 1932 up to October 24th, which date is quoted as the day on which the Company was officially wound-up.

On December 8th 1932, the creditors met in York to discuss the appointment of a Liquidator. The report of this meeting appeared in the *Yorkshire Evening Post* the following day, and by courtesy of the Editor I am able to quote it verbatim:-

"The creditors of the Sand Hutton Light Railway, which was incorporated under the Sand Hutton Light Railway Order 1920, and which ceased operations in June this year, met yesterday at the Office of the Official Receiver in York. It was decided not to apply for the appointment of a Liquidator, but to leave the estate in the hands of the Official Receiver.

"The summary statement of affairs showed gross liabilities amounting to £10,756. 5s. 3d., made up of preferential creditors for £50. 16s. 0d., and creditors for loans on debenture bonds, £10,705. 9s. 3d. The estimated value of the assets was £2,663. 16s. 3d., leaving a deficiency of £8,041. 12s. 9d. There was a called-up capital of £25,000 (in 2,500 shares of £10 each) which, together with the deficiency above, made a total of £33,041. 12s. 9d.

"The Order of the Light Railway Commissioners authorising the line was made in 1920 and the line itself was constructed on the Sand Hutton Estate to serve the villages of Sand Hutton, Claxton, Bossall, Buttercrambe and Scrayingham, to provide transport facilities for the tenants of Sir Robert Walker, Bart; and for the disposal of their agricultural produce, tillages, and feeding stuffs; and passenger services were also promoted for the convenience of residents in the district.

"The Company constructed a line 6 miles 46 chains in length, for goods traffic, and opened it in April, 1922, and of this, 4 miles 55 chains were opened for passenger traffic in 1924. They were worked continuously till June 1932. In June, 1923, £8,000 was borrowed on Debenture from two of the trustees of the Estate, and this and the interest is still owing.

"The line, which was a narrow gauge system connecting with the L.N.E.R. at Warthill, was equipped with two miniature locomotives, some passenger cars, and ample wagons. It was in the nature of a private undertaking, and was intended primarily for the benefit of those living on the Sand Hutton Estate. The whole of the capital, with the exception of twelve shares, was held by the trustees of the Sand Hutton Estate, and the whole of the Debentures were also held by trustees of the estate. In June last, the Ministry of Transport issued an order declaring that the Company should be wound-up.

"The causes of failure were given as— Decline in traffic owing to the close-down of Claxton Brickworks, acute agricultural depression in recent years and severe competition of road transport".

While the figures relating to the liabilities and estimated value of the assets, are probably correct, the references to the railway and rolling stock are obviously somewhat at variance with the established facts. Nevertheless, the report provides an illuminating insight into the state of the Company's affairs. (An almost identical report, but without rolling stock details, appeared in the *Yorkshire Gazette,* for December 16th, 1932, and a copy may be seen in the York Reference Library.)

It seems possible that in view of the shy nature of the line, the date of the actual last day of operation was not recorded in the press, nor have any notices of sale come to light. *The Railway Magazine* for October 1962, gives July 7th 1930, as the date on which the passenger service was finished—probably with the coach only. The M.O.T. returns for 1930 and 1931 both show that a few passengers were carried, and photographs indicate that they travelled in one of the wagons.

While it is seemingly impossible to pin-point the closing date, certain it is that Thos. W. Ward Ltd, of Sheffield, bought the railway for dismantling. They sent a foreman to Sand Hutton, and he recruited local labour to carry out the job, which was completed during 1933. Thus, the railway had a working life of 10 years—a brief existence indeed, and insufficient in fact for the course of the track and details of sidings to appear on the Ordnance Survey 6in or 1/2500 sheets, for the S.H.L.R. was built, operated and disappeared between revisions of these maps. This has made the preparation of accurate track lay-outs impossible. The general course of the line appeared on the more popular ½in to 1 mile sheets, and on the 1in to 1 mile sheets also. A Michelin road map of the late 1920's/early 1930's period does show the S.H.L.R. as in Dec. 1920—in 15in gauge form—from Warthill to Claxton Brickworks, and to Sand Hutton.

No. 11 is inspected by three visitors one day in 1932. George Batty, wearing his favourite trilby hat, is on the locomotive. This may have been the last run. (K.E. Hartley collection)

Chapter 12

SAND HUTTON PERSONALITIES

A group of passengers at Warthill about 1924-25. George Batty (in the peaked cap) stands on the coach balcony, and the L.N.E.R. stationmaster is on the right.
(K.E. Hartley collection)

No account of the S.H.L.R. can be considered complete without some reference to the people who, in one way or another, helped to operate the line, for The Hall, the railway, and Sand Hutton village were too intimately connected to be considered as separate entities. Next to Sir Robert Walker himself, without doubt the man most closely concerned with the railway was the late Mr. George L. Batty. He was born in Wensleydale, married at Thirsk Parish Church in 1889, and went to Sand Hutton a year later. There he served—uniquely—three Baronets of the Walker family: Sir Robert, his father and grandfather—and coped with the various mechanical affairs of the estate until his retirement in 1936. With equal versatility, he mended the young Baronet's model engines—as a boy Sir Robert spend much time with "Batty"—or, years later, took a major part in the building and operation of the Sand Hutton Light Railway. For a number of years he was in charge of the Estate Gas Plant and was Second Officer and Chief Engineer of the Sand Hutton Fire Brigade. When the miniature railway was laid down, this too became his responsibility, and in addition to being engine driver, he was the mainstay of the line.

After the 1914-18 War, when Sir Robert got busy with his scheme for the Sand Hutton Light Railway, Mr. Batty spent much time and frequent late nights, assisting with the plans, and indeed took a leading part in the project. He was not only the Engineer and Senior Driver, but also did a good deal of administrative work. Keen on sport, and a bowler of no mean ability, Mr. Batty was for some years very well known in local cricket circles, and was the mainstay of the Sand Hutton Club's attack. He maintained a lively interest in local cricket and tennis affairs until his decease in 1946. Friendly, imperturbable and well respected, he served Sir Robert Walker with a rare loyalty, and would allow no criticism of his master. On one occasion he saved the life of young Sir James Heron Walker (the present Baronet) when the latter fell into the lake—a thing long remembered by the boy.

Mrs. Batty, a native of North Kilvington, survived her husband by several years. Although of a somewhat retiring nature, she always gave the fullest support to all worthy local causes. When the "Buffet Service" operated on the Light Railway, Mrs. Batty saw to the supply of the necessary refreshments. These were served on the train by Miss A.G. Batty, one of her three daughters. Miss Batty taught in the local school for a number of years, and took an active part in village affairs. She died during the latter part of 1962, whilst this book was being prepared.

Although for a short time the S.H.L.R. was managed by Sir Robert's brother, Patrick, the line was officially managed from the Estate Office, by the late S.C. Foster, who was both Secretary and Manager. Mr. Foster started at the Estate Office as a clerk, and served in this capacity for some years before being appointed Estate Agent. In actual fact, however, it seems that much of the work connected with the railway, including paperwork, was done by Mr. Batty for Mr. Foster had much other business to keep him occupied. Also in the Estate Office, and concerned with the working of the line were Mr. J.C. Leeming and Mr. H. Leadhill, son of the Warthill Station Master at that time.

Mr. Fred Robinson was the other regular driver besides Mr. Batty. He started work on the railway at the age of 21, shortly before SYNOLDA was sent away. He was ably instructed by Mr. Batty in the running and care of the 18in gauge locomotives, and did much driving. As has been noted, he assisted in the demolition of the line. In later years, he worked at the W.D. Depot at Strensall but retired to Claxton for health reasons about 1958. Mr. Robinson's brother, Arthur, also worked on the S.H.L.R., and sometimes acted as Guard-Conductor on the passenger services. In the early days this position was filled by the late Mr. Johnson, who had retired some time previously from his post as Station Master at near-by Holtby. A dapper little figure in his uniform, Mr. Johnson is seen in several photographs.

In addition to those named above, the following also served on the Railway — Mr. H. Lindsay and his son Mr. G. Lindsay, Mr. A. Haigh, Mr. L. Dring and the late Mr. Charles Lindsay, who occasionally did a little driving. The standard working week was of 48 hours, and usually five or six men were employed on the line daily — 2 drivers, plus 3 or 4 loaders. The regular operating staff were provided with blue "pilot" overcoats and peaked caps bearing "S.H." badges; and while these were certainly worn, the most characteristic pictures of Mr. Batty invariably show him wearing a battered trilby of uncertain age, to which he was apparently much attached!

George Batty oiling round his locomotive for one of the last trips over the line.   (K.E. Hartley collection)

Fred Robinson, pictured outside his cottage in 1960, was a regular driver on the railway from 1922 until the closure.   (K.E. Hartley)

Chapter 13: PRESENT DAY

Despite the fact that when the first edition of *The Sand Hutton Light Rly* was published, in 1964, over 30 years had elapsed since the railway was dismantled, there were still a few relics to be seen, the largest of which was the old Depot building, easily visible from the road into Sand Hutton village. This was for many years used to house some of the implements used on a farm, but was also made to serve as a large poultry house, with an area of ground suitably wired-off to form chicken runs. Latterly, the shed had stood in splendid isolation in the midst of growing crops, gradually becoming more and more derelict, as no repairs were done to it over the years apart from several sloping buttresses being added to support the low brick base. By late 1964 half of the clerestory along the top of the Depot had fallen apart, and final collapse or demolition took place in the early part of 1965, leaving no trace. The coach body, over at Harton, also got steadily worse, but fortunately this was rescued just in time, and one can again travel in it—on the 60cm gauge Lincolnshire Coast Light Rly, at Humberston, near Cleethorpes, during the summer months. Close to the Depot site, the concrete piers and old standard gauge rails which supported the narrow gauge track were still mainly in position in 1978, and appeared likely to remain so; but the low embankment alongside the Depot, which led up to the bridge, was levelled-off many years ago, and the site of the bridge itself is becoming overgrown with saplings and bushes. In general, it is now difficult to discern very much of the route of the railway, except along the bridle path to White Sike, where one of the two small bridges, near White Sike cottages, remains in fair condition, although the second one, rather nearer to Warthill, was apparently overgrown and no longer visible. Warthill Station, though long without any main line track, still survives in good condition and occupied. The goods yard appears to be taken over by an industrial concern.

Of Sand Hutton Hall nothing remains, and the area around it is now quite unrecognisable, as it has become the site of a number of large, well screened houses. Part of the lake was still visible from a distance in 1978, but the parts of the estate remote from the former Hall and gardens appear to have been largely left to grow wild, and are fenced with barbed wire, supplemented by "Keep Out—Private" notices. All this is very different from the mid-1960's, when it was possible to go up to the Hall itself, and get some idea of the former beauty of the residence and its natural surroundings.

It should be stated that Lady Esmé did not remain at Sand Hutton after the death of Sir Robert, and since 1930 the Hall has been put to a variety of uses, and changed hands several times. It is understood that a local builder converted at least part of it into a number of flats, used by officers from Strensall Camp. Various other tenants have occupied parts of the Hall, and a section of the gardens was in use by a local smallholder, but by 1960 it had gradually become semi-derelict, and some portions (including the ballroom) had been demolished following the removal of all the carved woodwork. At the rear of the Hall, near the stables, the Coal House could still be seen in the mid-1960's; inside this building there still remained about fifteen feet of 18in gauge track embedded in the floor—the end of the short branch which served the Hall and Gardens. Also, the girders of the longer of the two bridges on the original 15in gauge line could still be seen spanning a corner of the lake. It is unlikely that anything now remains of these relics of Sir Robert's two railways.

Sand Hutton village did not appear to have changed since 1959-60, and seemed to retain its former quiet and peaceful lifestyle, but the local inhabitants, even at the Post Office-cum-Shop, were all strangers to me, for Mr. Leeming had died in 1964, and Fred Robinson passed away in 1970/71—his wife was then already deceased. This 1978 trip to Sand Hutton has not yet tempted me to re-visit the area, but mention may be made regarding the old village well—out of use for many years. It stands on a small patch of land near the Church, and had apparently become semi-derelict by about 1970. Hence it was restored to virtually its former well-kept appearance, apart from the bucket. But the restorers were looking ahead, as well as to the past, so at the bottom of the well, now dry, they placed the following items, for the interest of posterity—several coins, including the old half-crown, penny and halfpenny; a tape-recording of children's voices; photographs of local scenes; and a history of the old Sand Hutton Light Railway!

This should, logically, be the end of the story, but events over the past five years entail a regression to the 15in gauge Sand Hutton Railway. The history of SYNOLDA between 1922 and 1930 seems to be a combination of rumour and guesswork. However, although the local opinion was that she went to either Cumberland or Northumberland—incorrect in both cases it would seem—enquiry at Ravenglass revealed that she was not there, although *The Railway Magazine* for May 1932, contains a statement that the engine had been transferred to the Ravenglass & Eskdale Rly. Even as far back as 1927, when Mr. Household was preparing his article on the S.H.L.R. for *The Locomotive Magazine,* no information on the whereabouts of SYNOLDA was available. Commander N.G. Parkinson, who took over a 15in gauge railway at Southend in 1930, stated that he bought two locos of Bassett-Lowke origin for his line—a Class 10 and a Class 30. The Class 30, obtained from a garage

Sand Hutton Depot survived in use as a poultry shed in 1954. (K.E. Hartley)

The abutments and rail supports of the "Forth Bridge" near Sand Sutton Depot in 1954. (K.E. Hartley)

in Cricklewood, where it had been in store, was minus nameplates and number, but evidently still retained a feature not found on the other two examples of this class—the displacement lubricator between the frames, in front of the smokebox. The engine was in fact, SYNOLDA, and she was still at Southend when photographed by the late George Woodcock in 1938. He told me that the boiler had been to a firm in Rochester, and it had received new side and crown stays to the firebox.

The Southend line closed in 1938, and the locos and rolling stock were acquired by Mr. Dunn of Bishop Auckland, who sold them to Belle Vue, Manchester, about 1942. SYNOLDA received a new name—PRINCE CHARLES—some years later, but in 1964 was very crudely disguised to resemble an early American loco, for the 15in gauge Belle Vue Miniature Railway and had been renamed the Santa Fè Railroad! It was a monstrous insult to SYNOLDA, Henry Greenly and Bassett-Lowke, and a pretty poor compliment to H.R.H. to have such a lash-up bearing his name.

Happily, the *Ravenglass & Eskdale Railway Newsletter* No. 68, (Winter 1977/78) contained the very welcome report that SYNOLDA had been acquired by The Eskdale (Cumbria) Trust, and is now at Ravenglass! When the news reached Ravenglass that Trust House Forte had acquired Belle Vue, and were closing the railway, the R. & E.R. immediately contacted them, and were successful in obtaining the engine. In the end, Sir Charles Forte donated the locomotive to the Trust for display in the Railway Museum at Ravenglass. When found, the veteran loco was in a very sorry state—stripped down in the Belle Vue workshops. She was taken back to Ravenglass, where, after two seasons on static display in the Museum, she was given a general overhaul. In this work, thanks to the co-operation of British Nuclear Fuels Ltd., two of their engineering apprentices—David Clark and Robert Steel—were seconded to the R. & E.R. workshops and took a considerable part in the rebuild under the supervision of Ian Smith.

The boiler was found to be in good condition, having received attention in recent years. The chassis was stripped to the frames, the cylinders rebored (they are now 4¼in bore × 7in stroke), and the driving wheel tyres were widened and reprofiled, in addition to sundry lesser jobs. In deference to many requests, the original name of SYNOLDA was restored, and the firm of Bassett-Lowke, now kept busy with industrial model work, offered to make new builder's plates for the cab sides, to complete the job. The tender carries a brass plaque to commemorate the part taken by the apprentices in the restoration. Very appropriately, as elder sister to the R. & E.R.'s first 15in gauge loco—SANS PAREIL—SYNOLDA has been finished in the same beautiful blue livery, enhanced by the polished brass of the dome and safety-valve casings, and vermilion-painted side rods; the tender, too, bears another reminder of the early days of the 15in gauge period, for it is lettered N.G.R., as was that of SANS PAREIL. The whole restoration is a great credit to all who took part, and would indeed please both the designer and builders of these elegant engines.

One September 3rd 1980, SYNOLDA; driven by one of the apprentices hauled a special commissioning train from Irton Road to Ravenglass. The train carried Lord Wakefield and his guests, the Head of Reactors (Eric Slater) and the Head of Apprentice Training (Archie Spears), and the event was held both to confirm the re-birth of the locomotive, and as a "Thank you" to the staff at Windscale for their help in restoring it to full working order. Several other special runs were made before SYNOLDA returned to the Museum gallery, but from time to time she emerges to run up the line. Truly a very pleasant note on which to end!

SYNOLDA at Ravenglass following restoration to working order in 1980.

(Paul Ingham)

APPENDIX 1 SAND HUTTON LIGHT RAILWAY — TRAFFIC

Year	No. of Passengers Carried (3rd Class)	Goods Carried (Tons) General Merchandise and Minerals	Coal, Coke, Patent Fuel	Total Freight	Goods & Materials Carried (Tons) (Originating on Company's System) General	Coal etc.	Total	Milages Run by Engines Coaching Freight		Other Miles Light Running etc.	Total Engine Miles
1924	579	2,256	694	2,950	1,560	—	1,560	529	3,143	146	3,818
1925	2,185	3,175	1,453	4,628	1,264	—	1,264	1,918	3,480	153	5,551
1926	1,568	10,030	2,522	12,552	9,393	187	9,580	1,548	3,908	169	5,625
1927	1,534	10,306	3,039	13,345	9,903	29	9,932	1,485	4,225	252	5,962
1928	948	11,010	2,640	13,650	10,727	—	10,727	1,550	4,249	265	6,064
1929	791	3,946	2,300	6,246	3,522	—	3,522	1,460	3,856	232	5,548
1930	65	1,887	1,552	3,439	1,677	—	1,677	262	3,210	280	3,752
1931	61	570	295	865	493	—	493	18	2,074	249	2,341
1932	—	119/47	152	318	98	—	98	—	692	98	790

APPENDIX 2 SAND HUTTON LIGHT RAILWAY — RUNNING COSTS AND RECEIPTS

Year	Way & Works	Revenue Expenditure (In respect of Rly. Workings) Maintenance:- Rolling Stock Locos	Coach'g	Wagons	Loco. Running Expenses	Traffic	Total for year	Gross Receipts Freight	Passenger	Total	Moneys from separate business of Company: i.e. cultivation of land, etc.	Nett Receipts	Interest (Debentures)	Balance Carried Forward
	£	£ £	£	£	£	£	£	£	£	£	£	£	£	£
1924	13	70 —		5	134	142	459	502	12	514	—14	+ 41	254	— 112
1925	109	43 —		11	254	274	863	882	39*	921	+ 14	+ 73	309	— 305
1926	118	107 3		3	313	383	1107	1121	27	1148	+ 6	+ 47	350	— 557
1927	131	49 20		2	337	432	1153	1211	26	1237	+ 5	+ 89	360	— 779
		Rolling stock total												
1928	184		48		324	352	1104	1247	17	1264	—	+ 160	360	— 927
1929	119		22		238	315	855	807	15	866	—	+ 11	360	—1124
1930	106		41		159	239	703	503	1	504	—	— 199	360	—1734
1931	73		9		66	101	392	193	2	195	—	— 197	360	—2239
1932	22		6		35	49	172	65	—	65	—	— 107	293	—

*£1 taken for refreshments

From the Ministry of Transport Railway Returns 1924-1932.
The returns for 1932 are up to 24th October, the official date of winding-up of the Company.

BIBLIOGRAPHY

The following articles and books refer to the Sand Hutton Light Railway, or the earlier minature railway:

The Locomotive: 15 October 1928; 15th May 1942.
The Railway Magazine: January 1913; March 1914; May 1924; October 1924; May 1932; October 1962.
Models, Railways and Locomotives: December 1912; December 1913.
Model Railway News: September 1928.
Railways: April 1952.
Directory of Railway Officials & Year Book: (Issues 1924-32).
Light Railway Handbooks, No. 3 and No. 8: Kidner. (Oakwood Press)
Narrow Gauge Railways of Britain: Howson. (Ian Allan Ltd, 1948).
Light & Narrow Gauge Locomotives of Great Britain: Tonks (Birmingham Loco Club).
Service Suspended: Casserley (Ian Allan Ltd, 1952).
ABC Narrow Gauge Railways: Davies (Ian Allan Ltd, 1961).
Miniature Railways: Butterell (Ian Allan Ltd, 1966).
Miniature Steam Locomotives: Woodcock.
Miniature Railways, Vol 1: Clayton, Butterell and Jacot (Oakwood Press Ltd, 1971).
The Miniature World of Henry Greenly: Steel and Steel (M.A.P. Ltd, 1973).
The English Narrow Gauge Railway; Prideaux (David & Charles Ltd, 1979).
Railway Byways in Yorkshire: Redman (Dalesman Publishing, 1979).
Light Railways of Britain: Casserley (Bradford Barton).
The Ravenglass & Eskdale Railway: Davies (David & Charles Ltd, 1968).